Wind Surfing

Wind Surfing

Simon Bornhoft

US edition published by Stackpole Books

All inquiries should be addressed to
Stackpole Books
5067 Ritter Road
Mechanicsburg PA 17055

1 3 5 7 9 10 8 6 4 2

First Edition

ISBN 0-8117-3128-6 (pbk.)

Publisher: Mariëlle Renssen
Managing Editors: Claudia Dos Santos, Mari Roberts
Managing Art Editor: Peter Bosman
Editor: Sean Fraser
Designer and illustrator: Ben Latham
Production: Myrna Collins
Consultant: Peter Hart (UK)

Reproduction by Hirt & Carter (Cape) Pty Ltd
Printed and bound in Singapore by Craft Print (Pte) Ltd

Library of Congress Cataloging-in-Publication Data

Bornhoft, Simon
Windsurfing / Simon Bornhoft — 1st ed.
p. cm.
Includes index.
1. Windsurfing. 1. Title

GV811,63,W56 B67 2001

797.3'3—dc21   2001020149

Disclaimer

Author's acknowledgements
I would like to thank everyone who contributed towards this book, especially Sarah Fecher, the Professional Windsurfers Association, Boards magazine, Kath Newton and Gillian Horne of the Royal Yachting Association (UK), F2, Mistral, North, Bic & North, Gul Wetsuits, and the numerous photographers who provided the images for this book.

Dedication
For my daughter, Indi

Contents

Welcome to Windsurfing

What is it that makes windsurfing addictive and draws millions of people to lakes, harbors and coastlines around the world whenever the wind's up? For some, it is the sensation of sailing solely under the power of the wind, the exhilaration of high speed, the battle with the elements and the challenge of relying on personal technique and stamina. For others, it is the simple accessibility of the sport — it is really quite easy to learn. For many more, it is a relatively inexpensive and easy way to have fun on the water — be it at some exotic location or on your home territory.

Improved materials and modern designs mean that boards are more stable, while rigs are lighter and easier to handle, making learning considerably quicker and easier than when the sport first developed. Be warned, however, that at every level, windsurfing is active! It will make you fitter and stronger — although it's up to you how gentle or demanding you want it to be. There is no age requirement, and windsurfing is not about strength, Olympian fitness or having a technical mind.

Where did it all start?

Windsurfing was 'invented' in 1969 by Americans Jim Drake and Hoyle Schweitzer. The aim was to combine the wave-riding platform of a surfboard with the wind-harnessing power of a sail, using a unique universal joint so that the rig could be unsupported. The advantages were that although the concept demanded few ropes and technical features it had the capacity for high speed and maneuverability. In 1970, Schweitzer bought Drake's half of the partnership — much to Drake's regret as windsurfing developed into one of the world's most popular adventure sports.

The new sport was simpler than conventional sailing, requiring less time and skill to rig, and the board was easier to transport. The basic design and unique thrill resulted in a boom in the USA in the late 1970s, and by the following decade had spread throughout the world.

The first mass-produced board was the Windsurfer Regatta, moulded out of polyethylene plastic and filled with foam. The sails of colorful Dacron sailcloth slotted over a fiberglass mast. Wood was used on components such as the boom and dagger board. By modern standards, these boards were heavy and the rigs cumbersome, but that didn't detract from the enthusiasm.

While the original concept of the unsupported rig remains fundamental, pioneers have seen dramatic changes and advances. Boards have become smaller, lighter and more varied in application. They travel faster in less wind and allow newcomers to experience advanced techniques far sooner.

Today's boards can reach speeds of over 65kph (40 mph), ride waves the height of houses and jump 10m (35ft) in the air. The sport has full Olympic status, with a Professional Windsurfing Association world tour in male and female disciplines.

MOST ENTHUSIASTS ARE RECREATIONAL SAILORS, WITH LITTLE INTEREST IN COMPETITIVE WINDSURFING.

Opposite ADVANCES IN THE DEVELOPMENT OF SAILS AND RIGS MEANS THAT WINDSURFING IS NOW EASIER.

Getting

Equipped

In terms of components, windsurfing is essentially a simple sport, the main parts being a board and a rig (the collective term for sail, mast, boom and mast base that connects to the board). Selecting the most suitable model from the huge number available can, however, appear daunting to the newcomer. This equipment guide will explain the right equipment to learn on and highlight the important points to bear in mind when purchasing your first board.

Basic equipment

It is vital to use equipment suited to your level of ability and to have it set it up correctly. Otherwise you will end up being challenged by the conditions and not enjoying the sport as much as you should. It's advisable to spend your first few hours or days on a board that you have hired from a recognized center. If you decide to purchase a board and rig, ask the retailer to help you rig it correctly; and, whenever possible, sail with , more experienced sailors who understand how the equipment works. This will save you a lot of time and effort.

above WINDSURFING EQUIPMENT — FOR ALL LEVELS, BUILDS AND AGES — IS NOW LIGHTER AND EASIER TO USE THAN EVER BEFORE.

opposite MODERN, 'WIDESTYLE' BEGINNER SHORT BOARDS ARE SO EASY AND STABLE TO SAIL, YOU CAN DO ALMOST ANYTHING ON THEM.

The long and short of it

Windsurfing is divided into two distinct categories: long-board sailing and short-board sailing. In principle, long boards are suited to beginners in light winds and on flat water. However, once the wind strength approaches and passes the Force 3/4, windsurfing becomes a planing sport, allowing you to travel at greater speed. This opens up a new set of challenges that require more advanced techniques and changes in equipment. While it is acceptable to continue using long boards in stronger winds, most recreational sailors find it easier and more enjoyable to progress to smaller boards. When a board is travelling at greater speeds, it requires less volume to support the sailor. At the same time, the high volume and size of long boards is a disadvantage in choppy, wind-whipped water, especially in exposed coastal areas. There used to be a large gap between the long and short boards, but today board ranges are so extensive that there are a range of boards available which allow you to gradually progress to smaller boards. In time you too will be able to venture onto smaller boards, but for now it's best to use equipment designed for the beginners.

The board

Important factors when selecting a board are volume and width. During the early stages, you need maximum stability and ease, so aim for a wide board (for stability) with a high volume (to aid buoyancy). Known as long boards, these offer a stable platform on which to practice. While you may be tempted to have a go on a short board, it will semi-submerge when you stand on it and be harder to balance, making learning difficult. There is a great deal of fun to be had on a long board and many of your skills can be perfected in lighter winds.

Most beginner boards have between 160—240l (280—420pts) of volume and are 60—70cm (23—28 inches) wide. Heavy men should go for maximum volume, while women and children may opt for smaller boards.

Boards have a foam core and an outer skin of blown moulded polyethylene or a composite material.

■ Blown-moulded boards are tough, but heavy.

■ Composite boards comprise layers of materials, such as fiberglass, carbon and Kevlar, bonded by epoxy resin.

■ More expensive boards have a 'honeycomb sandwich' laid between the inner core and outer coating.

Buying your first board

To master basic maneuvers, hire a board designed for beginners; once you are able to balance, uphaul the rig, sail in a straight line and turn round again, then buy your own board. It should be stable and versatile enough for most conditions and enable you to progress through all techniques. Even if your aim is to sail short boards, long boards can be kept for light winds.

ALL-ROUND BOARDS OFFER BOTH STABILITY AND VOLUME FOR BEGINNERS. THEY ALSO HAVE FOOTSTRAPS TO INCREASE THEIR VERSATILITY FOR STRONGER WINDS AND MORE EXPERIENCED SAILORS.

■ The best option is an all-round design. It has slightly less volume and width than an absolute beginner's board, but offers greater versatility. It has a dagger board, mast track (sliding or fixed) and footstraps (remove these until you are able to use them).

■ 'Widestyle' beginner's boards don't have a dagger board and are shorter, usually less than 3m (9ft). What they lack in length they make up in volume and width, so they look short and fat. They are suited to strong winds and introduce newcomers to planing conditions on a wide, stable platform. Basic techniques are the same as on longer boards. Instructors will advise on the board best suited to your location and level of skill.

Getting to know your board

Knowing your board well — and what you are capable of doing — will help build confidence out on the water.

■ Nose Boards with lower volume in the nose are harder to sail and submerge more easily, so try to learn on a board with a wider nose.

■ Tail Boards with narrow tails may tip and are suited to strong winds where speed gives the board stability.

■ Non-slip coating All boards have non-slip coating to prevent your feet sliding around on the deck.

■ Dagger board The dagger board helps the beginner to sail closer to the wind, reducing the chances of drifting downwind and away from the starting point.

■ Fin The fin provides lateral and directional stability. For beginners or intermediates on all-round boards, a 30—40cm (12—16 inches) fin will suit most conditions.

■ Mast track The mast track is where the rig base attaches to the board. The position of the rig on the mast track can be altered to suit conditions and points of sail, but beginners should keep the mast base in the middle of the track (see Basic Assembly on page 20).

The rig

With practice, it takes five minutes to prepare a sail. Once assembled, you have your own power source which pivots around the universal joint. The rig can be moved in a three-dimensional way when attached to the board — this enables you to turn the board anywhere you wish and at whatever pace the wind dictates.

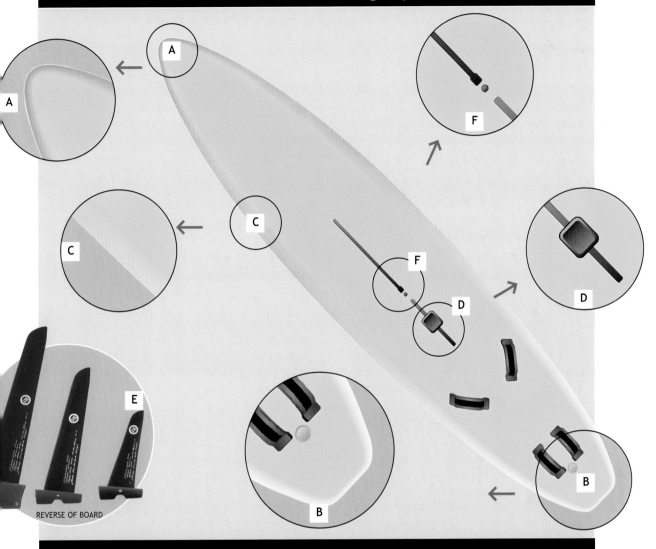

REVERSE OF BOARD

A NOSE: THE NOSE HAS TO RISE OUT OF THE WATER AS YOU SAIL ALONG TO ALLOW THE BOARD TO PASS OVER SMALL WAVES AND ACCELERATE WITHOUT NOSE-DIVING.

B TAIL: THE TAIL OF THE BOARD ALWAYS STAYS IN THE WATER AND HAS SHARPER RAILS (EDGES) THAN THE REST OF THE BOARD TO HELP THE BOARD RELEASE WATER MORE QUICKLY OFF THE TAIL AND THUS ACCELERATE. THE WIDE TAIL OFFERS STABILITY AND HELPS YOU MOVE BACK ON THE BOARD WITHOUT SINKING.

C NON-SLIP COATING: ALL BOARDS ARE COVERED WITH A NON-SLIP COATING THAT FEELS LIKE SANDPAPER AND PROVIDES RESISTANCE.

D DAGGER BOARD LEVER: A DAGGER BOARD IS THE DEFINING FEATURE OF A LONG BOARD AND CAN BE USED IN THE 'DOWN' POSITION OR RETRACTED UP IN TO THE HULL. WHEN THE DAGGER BOARD IS DOWN, IT ACTS LIKE A KEEL ON A BOAT, PROVIDING EXTRA STABILITY AND MAKING IT EASIER TO TURN THE BOARD AROUND.

E FIN: WITHOUT A FIN, THE BOARD WOULD SIMPLY SPIN AROUND IN CIRCLES. FINS ARE MOULDED OUT OF REINFORCED GLASS FIBER (FINS OF G10 ARE THE TOUGHEST) AND SLOT INTO THE 'FIN BOX' ON THE UNDERSIDE OF THE BOARD, CLOSE TO THE REAR. THE FIN IS HELD IN A FIXED POSITION BY A 'FIN BOLT' THAT SCREWS THROUGH FROM THE DECK.

F MAST TRACK: THERE ARE TWO DISTINCT TYPES OF MAST TRACK FITTINGS: FIXED AND ADJUSTABLE. THE FIXED TRACK — NOW THE MOST WIDELY USED — COMPRISES A GROOVED TRACK IN THE MIDDLE OF THE BOARD. THE RIG IS ATTACHED BY A 'DECK PLATE', WHICH CAN BE POSITIONED ANYWHERE IN THE TRACK WITH A SCREW AND NUT. ONCE TIGHTENED, IT REMAINS IN ONE POSITION.

The sail

Windsurfing sails comprise panels that are taped and sewn together to give the sail its shape. They are made from a combination of monofilm (a clear PVC film) and colored Dacron (woven polyester).

The sail is supported by fiberglass rods known as battens, which are fixed semi-permanently in tight-fitting batten pockets. The battens give the sail rigidity, from the luff (front of the sail) to the leech (trailing edge of the sail). When the board changes direction, the battens rotate around the mast, ensuring that they always lie on the leeward side of the mast, which is the most aerodynamic shape. A sail with 4–5 battens is ideal for entry level.

Sail sizes

The choice of sail size is determined by the sailor's body weight, ability and the wind conditions. The heavier you are, the more sail you will need to harness the wind, while the greater the wind speed the smaller the sail required. This is because, as wind speed increases, so will the power in the sail, requiring more effort and technique to control it. Sailing 'over-powered' — when the sail becomes too big for the wind strength — is tiring, difficult, and can be dangerous. Moving down in sail size is known as 'changing down'. Conversely, if the wind suddenly subsides, the power in the sail can be too little to balance against. This is usually the time to 'change up'.

Absolute beginners are usually taught on small sails (3–5m/10–16ft) to facilitate handling. Once the basics have been grasped, a good all-round size on a long board is about 5.5–6.5m (18–21ft), which can be used in winds up to Force 4.

Sail types

■ Race sails are performance-oriented for straight-line sailing at speed. Made in the larger sizes, they are designed for maximum power and identifiable by large luff tubes, long booms, lower foot shapes and a large number of battens (two of which are below boom height).

■ All-round, no-cam or wave-slalom sails are largely for recreational use, offering a compromise between power and maneuverability. Common features are the five or six battens and a shape that falls between that of 'race' sails and 'wave' sails.

■ Wave sails are easier to maneuver in rough conditions. They have shorter booms, fewer battens and a higher cut foot shape.

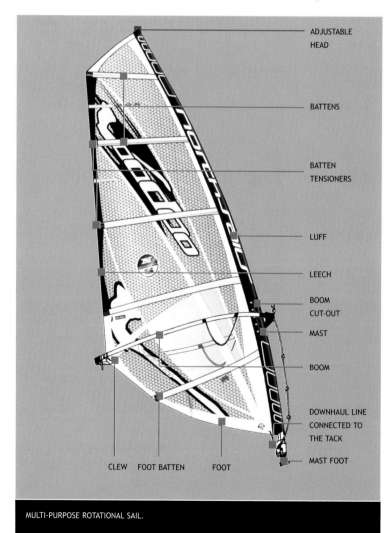

ADJUSTABLE HEAD · BATTENS · BATTEN TENSIONERS · LUFF · LEECH · BOOM CUT-OUT · MAST · BOOM · DOWNHAUL LINE CONNECTED TO THE TACK · MAST FOOT · CLEW · FOOT BATTEN · FOOT

MULTI-PURPOSE ROTATIONAL SAIL.

Race sail	Free-ride sail	Wave sail
■ Large luff tube	■ Medium luff tube	■ Narrow luff tube
■ 4–5 camber inducers	■ No camber inducers	■ No camber inducer
■ 6–8 battens	■ 5–7 battens	■ 4–6 battens
■ Low-footed shape	■ Medium low-foot shape	■ High-cut foot shape, short boom

Masts

Most modern masts come in two pieces for easy storage, and are usually made of epoxy fiberglass with varying degrees of carbon. The higher the carbon content of the mast, the lighter the mast. For most recreational sailing, a carbon content of 30–50 per cent is perfectly adequate. Anything higher than this is simply a luxury, but if you are prepared to pay the money, it is possible to buy a 75–100 per cent carbon mast that weighs only 2kg (4½ pounds). Windsurfing masts vary in length and enthusiasts may have a number of masts to match each of their sails, but for most beginners one mast can fit up to three sails. Sail manufacturers print the recommended mast length on the foot of the sail, so always check that you have the right size mast for the sail you are using, or you may find that rigging it is impossible.

Mast extensions

A mast extension allows you to adjust the mast length to fit the sail exactly, and you are able to 'change up' to a bigger sail with only a few minor adjustments.

Booms

The boom is usually made of aluminium, making it strong enough to carry your body weight as you hang off it. For comfort, every boom is covered with a textured grip. The boom attaches to the mast with a simple reinforced plastic clamp and attaches to the sail at the other (clew) end with a piece of rope that loops through an eyelet in the sail. To accommodate the differences in sail sizes, booms have a telescopic 'back end' that allows you to adjust the boom length to fit your sail. Sails have recommended boom lengths printed on them to enable you to extend the boom to the right length.

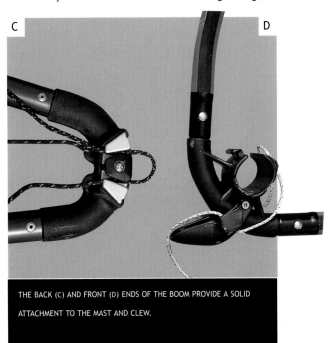

A THE MASTS MAY LOOK THE SAME, BUT THEY COME IN MANY SIZES AND CHARACTERISTICS TO SUIT A WIDE SELECTION OF SAILS.
B MAST EXTENSIONS ENABLE THE MAST LENGTH TO BE INCREASED OR DECREASED TO FIT SAILS OF DIFFERENT SIZES.

THE BACK (C) AND FRONT (D) ENDS OF THE BOOM PROVIDE A SOLID ATTACHMENT TO THE MAST AND CLEW.

Accessories

Wetsuits

Some kind of body covering is always necessary to protect you from the rays of the sun or cold temperatures, and to cushion your body should you fall. Wetsuits come in many different thicknesses, and styles and offer varying degrees of cover. The cooler the air and water temperature, the greater the thickness and cover required.

■ In northern European locations, with cool winds and chilly waters, the $^1/_5$-inch full-bodied Steamer is a popular choice from autumn through to spring. Once the air and water temperature warm up in the summer months, enthusiasts will wear a 3mm ($^1/_{10}$ inch) short-arm Steamer.

■ In southern European summers, southern hemisphere locations and tropical climates, the need for a full-length wetsuit is not always necessary, but even in very hot, sunny climates you have to be careful. Being out on the sea, often submerged and always exposed to the breeze, you are vulnerable to 'wind chill'. It is thus quite common to see windsurfers wearing a 2–3mm ($^1/_{12}$–$^1/_{10}$ inch) 'shortie' wetsuit in these climates.

Shoes and boots

Windsurfing can be hard on the feet, so keep them protected. Surf shoes for warm water, or wetsuit boots for colder climes, are designed for the job. They have a good grip, are flexible and provide protection against objects on the board – such as the dagger board and the mast base – as well as natural hazards, such as rocks and stones, when transporting the board to and from the water.

Buoyancy aids

While wetsuits provide you with buoyancy, beginners should wear a buoyancy jacket. This will safeguard you in the early stages when you are in the water frequently. Make sure it fits well and is not damaged.

Gloves

Uphauling the sail and hanging off the boom can be hard on your hands. Gloves protect the skin but restrict your grip and can thus tire the forearms quickly. You might prefer not to use them – it will be painful to begin with, but your hands will toughen up. If you do use gloves, make sure they are windsurfing or sailing gloves. Gloves stretch when wet, so choose the lightest, thinnest and tightest-fitting pair you can find.

A WETSUITS CATER FOR ALL BODY BUILDS AND CLIMATES.

B ALTHOUGH MANY WINDSURFERS MAY CHOOSE NOT TO WEAR BOOTS, THEY DO PROVIDE WARMTH IN COLDER WATERS.

C SURF SHOES PROVIDE GRIP AND PROTECT FEET FROM ROCKS AND REEFS.

D BEGINNERS SHOULD ALWAYS WEAR BUOYANCY JACKETS.

E GLOVES MAY PROTECT HANDS – AND ESPECIALLY PALMS – FROM INJURY.

Harnesses

A harness will be of no use in the first stages of learning, but it will eventually become an essential part of your windsurfing, taking the strain off your arms and helping you to control the rig in stronger winds and at faster speeds. A harness line is a fixed length of line that attaches to each side of the boom, just between your hands, to which you attach the harness hook. While you are free to disconnect at anytime, you are temporarily attached to the rig, so it is important to have a good grasp of the basics — or you will go where the rig goes!

Three types

■ The seat or slalom harness fits round the backside and two straps pass between the legs. This is the most popular option for recreational sailors who are looking for control at speed or who are new to harnessing.

■ The waist harness has a slightly higher hook — just above the belly button — and fits round the waist and lower back. It provides back support and encourages more upright sailing suitable for maneuvers, such as sailing in waves. This harness is increasingly the choice of all levels of short-board sailors intent on easy manoeuvring.

■ The chest harness — once standard — is now only used by experienced windsurfers who like the ease of hooking in and out as well as the protection the high back gives when landing incorrectly on dynamic moves.

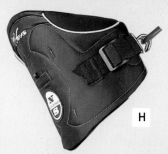

H

Buying a harness

A new harness should fit snugly and be easy to tighten and adjust. There are specific designs for women and children and a good retailer will be able to help you find the right fit and style for your sailing.

Roof rack and straps

It is quite likely that you will be using a vehicle to transport your windsurfer to the water. If this is the case, make sure you have a solid roof rack and that the board is securely fixed to the roof. Never use ropes (they damage equipment) or elastic 'bungee' cords (they are not secure enough and are thus dangerous). Proper windsurfing roof-rack straps are strong and have safe, easily adjustable buckles to fix the board and rig to the roof rack.

G

F

I

F THIS SEAT, OR SLALOM, HARNESS HAS A BACK SUPPORT.

G A STANDARD SEAT HARNESS SITS AROUND THE HIPS, BUT HAS LIMITED BACK SUPPORT.

H A WAIST HARNESS PROVIDES BACK SUPPORT AND GIVES AN UPRIGHT STANCE, WHICH IS FAVORED FOR A MORE RELAXED STYLE OF SAILING.

I ROOF RACKS WITH STRONG STRAPS ALLOW BOARDS TO BE TRANSPORTED.

Getting
Started

to get started, you will need access to a safe waterway, a beginner's board and rig, and a good understanding of the basic techniques of windsurfing. The easiest and safest way to start is in an enclosed waterway — and with professional instruction. There are thousands of recognized windsurfing schools and centers around the world offering assistance to those taking up the sport. It is not advisable to buy equipment until you have actually tried to windsurf. If you decide to take a course, you can hire suitable equipment. As you become more experienced, you can start to select equipment to help your progress.

A course will get you started, but it takes time and practice to get the most out of windsurfing. You will find that success comes with an understanding of the skills involved, choosing the right conditions and equipment — and spending plenty of time getting wet.

Be prepared
Basic preparation and safety checks must precede your first session. There is plenty of good equipment for beginners, but how it is prepared is vital. Good rigging and set-up will give you the best starting point.

Only once you have mastered the essentials are you ready to tackle basic theories behind how a sail works and other techniques that will enable you to sail, steer and turn, as well as react to the wind. Be sure to employ a good instructor and take the time to master the simple pointers. This will help you to avoid picking up bad habits that will slow your progress later on.

Rigging and set-up
Every sailor, irrespective of ability, requires control, stability, lightness in the hands and a wide wind range from their sail. This is only achievable when a sail is correctly rigged and the board and rig are set up properly (see Correcting a badly rigged sail on page 22) — otherwise the gear will work against you, not respond properly to the wind, dismantle on the water or break.

Preparing the board and rig
Basic preparation will apply to every board and sail you own. You can practice rigging on your own, but when it comes to taking the board onto the water for the first time, ask an experienced sailor to check the gear and even try it out for you.

ALWAYS TAKE INSTRUCTION FROM A QUALIFIED INSTRUCTOR AT A RECOGNIZED WINDSURFING CENTER. WITH THE HELP OF EXPERIENCED TEACHERS, YOU WILL PROGRESS FAR MORE RAPIDLY.

opposite INITIAL SUCCESS ON THE WATER WILL DEPEND NOT ONLY ON SKILL, BUT ALSO ON AN UNDERSTANDING OF BASIC SAILING THEORIES.

The right size sail

As you gain more experience on the water, you will find that you are able to handle bigger sails. After a few days, it may even be possible to use 4.5–5.5m (15–18ft) sails in light to moderate winds (below 12 knots or 22kph/14mph). During your initial sessions, choose the smallest, most manageable sail. A 4–4.5m (13–15ft) sail suits most conditions.

Wind strength

Wind strength is an important factor in deciding on sail size. The stronger the wind, the smaller the sail, so learn to judge wind speed. There are hand-held wind-speed indicators that tell you the precise strength of the wind, but it is also important to be able to 'read' the conditions on your own.

■ Look at the texture of the water's surface. You may never have noticed it before but now, looking into the wind on the water, you will see that the wind makes 'fish scale' ripples on the surface. As the wind increases in strength, the intensity and density of these 'fish scales' becomes more obvious. As the wind really freshens, white caps will appear. This is a good sign that it's too windy for beginners. Ideally, you want relatively smooth, calm water and winds between 3–10 knots.

■ There are also useful signs to look out for on land. Smoke rising straight up will mean a gentle day on the water. Conversely, swaying trees and swooshing leaves will be a clear indication that the conditions might be too much for you to handle.

■ Talk to other windsurfers; they will be able to help match the sail to the conditions. 'What are they using out there?' is a phrase heard at windsurfing locations around the world. Even professional windsurfers ask, so don't feel awkward doing so yourself.

Body weight and ability

Besides wind strength, body weight and personal ability are defining factors in the choice of sail size. The heavier and more experienced you are, the bigger the sail you are able to use. So, if you are light and new to the sport, you should be using a smaller sail than other windsurfers in the same conditions. Based on what other windsurfers are using and your previous experiences in similar conditions, it won't take long to be able to choose the right sail for you.

Basic assembly

The basic components and method of rigging and preparation are the same, no matter what brand of board or sail you have. Find a sheltered place to rig your equipment. Never leave it half rigged or unattended. The slightest breeze can send a rig flying. Always make sure that the rig is secured to the board or something solid, like your car or a fence post, if you do need to leave it.

SAILS COME IN DIFFERENT SIZES TO SUIT THE WIND'S STRENGTH AND THE SAILOR'S WEIGHT AND ABILITY. THE AVERAGE SAIL RANGE IS 4M–8M (13FT–26FT).

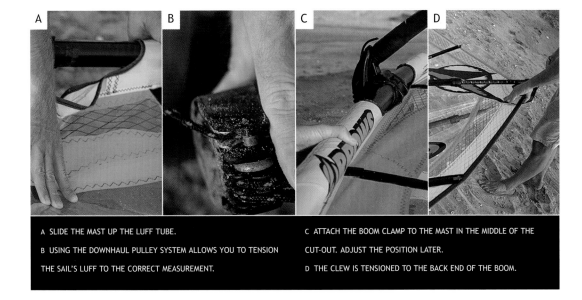

A SLIDE THE MAST UP THE LUFF TUBE.

B USING THE DOWNHAUL PULLEY SYSTEM ALLOWS YOU TO TENSION THE SAIL'S LUFF TO THE CORRECT MEASUREMENT.

C ATTACH THE BOOM CLAMP TO THE MAST IN THE MIDDLE OF THE CUT-OUT. ADJUST THE POSITION LATER.

D THE CLEW IS TENSIONED TO THE BACK END OF THE BOOM.

Assembling your rig

Before you start assembling the rig, you need to familiarize yourself with its components (see pages 13 and 14) and their functions.

Step 1 First, slide the mast up the luff tube of the sail. When the mast reaches the top of the sail, put the mast extension into the bottom of the mast and attach it to the sail's cringle or eyelet, using the downhaul pulley block. Check your manufacturer's measurements on the sail to make sure that the combined mast length and extension length matches the sail's recommended luff length (see page 94).

Step 2 The sail attains its shape by 'putting on the downhaul'. This involves a rather physical action, so wrap the downhaul (see page 94) around a suitable handle (known as a 'grunt') and, with your foot pushing against the mast base, pull on the downhaul rope until the bottom of the sail almost touches the bottom of the mast base. If you read the measurements correctly, this should leave a small gap (2.5–5cm/1–2 inches) for fine-tuning.

Step 3 Attach the boom's front end to the mast, roughly in the middle of the cutout in the sail. It is important to get a solid fixing, so make sure that the clamp is tight and firmly in position on the mast.

Step 4 Thread the outhaul line through the cringle at the end of the sail. Check the manufacturer's recommended measurements on the sail and set the boom length to match. Just like the downhaul, you will have a range of settings for fine-tuning. Most modern sails need some tension to help give them shape and stability. When set correctly, the sail reaches the end of the recommended boom length.

Step 5 The battens will already be in the sail, but check for excessive crinkles along the batten pockets. If there are any, use the batten tensioners at the leech to tighten the batten and remove the creases.

Step 6 Slot the dagger board into its casing. Many brands have these permanently fitted, so you might find that it is already in place. Check that the dagger board can be easily adjusted, and then leave it retracted into the board until you are on the water.

Step 7 Fit the mast base into the track to make the board easier to carry. The mast track will have a variation in the settings, but for most beginners on all-round boards the mast track is best positioned in the middle of the track – 145–165cm (57–65 inches) from the tail. Make sure it is fitted securely.

Step 8 Ensure that the fin is screwed tightly into the fin box and that everything is secure.

THE SAIL HAS AN AIRFOIL SHAPE AND THE LUFF SLEEVE IS TAUT AROUND THE BOOM AREA. THE BATTEN ABOVE THE BOOM LIES ON ONE SIDE OF THE MAST, SO THAT IT CAN FREELY ROTATE ACROSS THE MAST WHEN THE SAIL FILLS WITH WIND FROM THE OTHER SIDE. THE CLEW IS HELD IN PLACE.

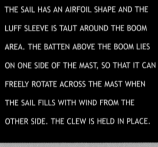

Correcting a badly rigged sail

There are many pitfalls in rigging a sail, but once you are aware of the correct procedure, you should be able to avoid problems on the water.

Each manufacturer will provide a set of rigging instructions for their particular sail, and yet, although there are differences between brands, all sails respond to the basic rigging principles. The idea is to encourage a creaseless, stable airfoil shape. Below are some of the common problems you may encounter when tuning your sail.

A badly rigged sail

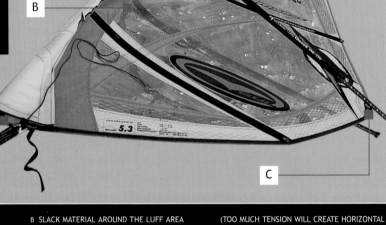

A THE SAIL IS BAGGY AND THERE ARE HORIZONTAL CREASES ACROSS THE SAIL. TO SOLVE THIS, INCREASE THE TENSION ON THE DOWNHAUL. IF YOU HAVE NO ROOM TO DO THIS, EXTEND THE MAST EXTENSION AND REAPPLY MORE DOWNHAUL UNTIL ALL THE CREASES ARE REMOVED. IT IS DIFFICULT TO PUT ON TOO MUCH DOWNHAUL, BUT IF THE SAIL IS COMPLETELY FLAT AND THE BATTEN ABOVE THE BOOM COMES AWAY AT RIGHT ANGLES FROM THE MIDDLE OF THE MAST, THEN THE SAIL MIGHT HAVE TOO MUCH DOWNHAUL.

B SLACK MATERIAL AROUND THE LUFF AREA ALSO MEANS THERE IS INSUFFICIENT DOWNHAUL ON THE SAIL, MAKING IT UNSTABLE AND LESS SENSITIVE TO THE EFFECTS OF THE WIND. IF YOU ARE ABLE TO MOVE IT WITH YOUR HAND THEN IT IS TOO LOOSE. IT SHOULD FEEL TIGHT AND IMMOVABLE.

C THE CLEW SHOULD BE TENSIONED SO THE SAIL DOES NOT TOUCH THE BOOM'S SIDES. THE BOOM SHOULD BE EXTENDED SO THAT THE SAIL'S CLEW JUST REACHES THE END. A GAP WILL MAKE THE BOOM AND SAIL UNSTABLE.

(TOO MUCH TENSION WILL CREATE HORIZONTAL CREASES RUNNING FROM THE CLEW AND FAN-LIKE CREASES FROM THE BOOM END.)

D SET THE SAIL BOTTOM AS CLOSE TO THE MAST BASE AS POSSIBLE. ADJUST THE MAST EXTENSION TO ALLOW ENOUGH DOWNHAUL TO BE APPLIED AND TO AVOID LARGE GAPS.

E MOVEMENT IN THE BOOM'S ATTACHMENT TO THE MAST MEANS IT IS LIKELY TO SLIP DOWN OR COME OFF WHILE SAILING. A TIGHT BOOM IS SAFER AND GIVES YOU A BETTER FEEL FOR THE RIG AND THE WIND.

Tuning

The bigger the sail, the more powerful it will be, but the sail's power is also governed by its 'fullness' (the amount of belly, or curve, in the sail). A sail rigged for light winds should be set fuller (in other words, with more belly). As the wind increases, the sail should be set flatter, making it easier to control. To adjust the fullness in a sail, use the downhaul and outhaul (see pages 94 and 95). The more downhaul and outhaul you apply, the flatter the sail becomes. The manufacturers' recommended settings are printed on each sail, but be sure to check that the amount of outhaul is never more than just a simple tug of 3–5cm (1$\frac{1}{5}$–2 inches) to hold the clew in place. Remember that if the wind picks up, always use downhaul first to flatten the sail; only then may the outhaul be tightened up.

Tools of the trade

It is virtually impossible to obtain enough downhaul without the aid of a pulley system. A ratio of 4:1 (the number of times the rope passes through the pulley blocks) is a minimum, 6:1 is ideal and 8:1 is a luxury. A rope that has been passed through an eyelet is entirely unacceptable. The other vital tool is, of course, the 'grunt'. Mast feet, easy rigs, harness hooks and boom tubing will all save your back and hands when applying the downhaul.

USING THE GRUNT ENABLES YOU TO APPLY PLENTY OF TENSION TO THE DOWNHAUL AND ALSO PREVENTS THE LINE FROM CUTTING INTO THE PALMS OF YOUR HANDS.

Adjusting the boom height

It is important to position the boom at the right height for your personal height. With the mast base inserted in the extension, hold the mast upright on solid ground. The boom clamp should rest between your shoulder and chin. To adjust it, release the boom clamp and slide the boom into position – to shoulder level – and secure the clamp. Having the boom correctly positioned makes a big difference to your ability to control and sail the board properly. If it is too low or too high, you will waste energy and thus hinder your progression.

HAVING THE BOOM TOO LOW REDUCES CONTROL OVER THE RIG AND DRAMATICALLY HINDERS YOUR TECHNIQUE, ESPECIALLY WHEN YOU ARE TRYING TO MASTER THE HARNESS AND STRONGER WINDS.

THE BOOM CLAMP SHOULD BE POSITIONED SO THAT IT LIES AT APPROXIMATELY SHOULDER AND CHIN HEIGHT WHEN THE RIG IS BEING HELD UPRIGHT.

Carrying your equipment

Getting the board and rig down to the water's edge for the first time can mean all sorts of problems. Suddenly, you are faced with two large cumbersome objects. Out of the wind, they are quite light to handle, but even the slightest breeze can make it difficult getting them to the shore. The trick is to get the board close to the water's edge before rigging up. If it is some distance between the rigging area and the sailing area, never leave the rig unattached or exposed to the wind — it might not be there by the time you get back. Carry the board first and leave the rig in a sheltered area or use an uphaul to tie it to something solid until you can go back for it. The rig should then be attached to the board as soon as possible — rigs travel faster than humans and other beach users are at serious risk from flying rigs. Don't turn away — even for only a few seconds. Once attached, use the board as an anchor by placing

it upwind. The weight of the board holds the rig down and forces the wind to pass over the rig, reducing the chances of it being flipped about. Ideally, the rig should be oriented so that the wind is passing up the rig, from mast base towards the mast tip. Only then may the whole set-up be left for as long as you wish.

Carrying the board

To carry the board, put the dagger board in the down position so that you can get your hand into the dagger board casing, or even hold onto the dagger board itself (which is usually a good balancing point). Your other hand can hold onto the mast track or mast base on the other side of the board. When possible, try to point the nose or tail into the wind. If the side of the board faces the wind, you'll be caught by gusts and spun round. Leave it by the shoreline with the dagger board retracted and with the tail pointing directly into the wind. If you are on a sandy beach, push the fin into the sand to secure the board while you fetch the rig.

TO CARRY THE BOARD TO AND FROM THE WATER, HOLD THE BOARD AT YOUR SIDE, WITH ONE HAND ON THE MAST TRACK AND THE OTHER ON THE DAGGER BOARD.

Carrying the rig

Always use the wind to your advantage. Keeping the mast foot and/or mast facing the wind ensures that the wind passes over the sail, making it lighter and more stable. Choose the option you find easiest in the conditions. You may need to try different carrying positions, depending on the specific wind conditions at play.

Carrying the rig above your head

The rig should be carried horizontally, with the mast perpendicular to the wind — ideally with the mast base pointing in the direction of travel. This allows the wind underneath the sail and helps it to fly. The rig is stable and controllable if the wind passes over the mast first. If you turn the rig so that the wind blows across the back of the sail, it becomes heavy and will flip over. In light winds, carry the rig above your head. One hand holds the mast, and the other the boom. The head forms the third part of the triangle and rests gently on the sail. In this configuration, try to take most of the weight on your arms, or you risk damaging the sail.

Carrying the rig by your side

A common method of carrying in strong winds or short distances is to have the rig at hip level. The mast foot points into the wind, the front hand holds the boom and the back hand the mast. The rig is lifted and rested on the hip. If the rig is level and the mast is perpendicular to the wind, the breeze will lift the sail for you.

Carrying the board and rig together

If you aren't far from the water's edge, you can carry the board and rig at the same time. Flip the board on its side so that the board is at 90°, resting on its edge. To find the balance point, place your back hand on the boom, hold the tail of the board or back footstrap, and push the nose along the ground. Provided you are on sand or light shingle, you should not damage the board.

Wind direction

The red arrows that feature on photographs throughout this book indicate wind direction.

WHEN YOU ARE CARRYING THE RIG ABOVE YOUR HEAD, POINT THE MAST AND THE MAST BASE INTO THE WIND. THIS METHOD IS MOST COMMONLY USED IN LIGHT WIND CONDITIONS.

IN STRONGER WINDS, OR FOR SHORT DISTANCES, IT MAY BE EASIER TO CARRY THE RIG AT YOUR SIDE, ONCE AGAIN WITH THE MAST FOOT AND/OR MAST POINTING INTO THE WIND.

IT IS POSSIBLE TO CARRY BOTH THE BOARD AND RIG TOGETHER FOR SHORT DISTANCES, WITH SMALLER AND LIGHTER BOARDS BEING HELD COMPLETELY OFF THE GROUND.

Learning the basics

For your first few times on the water, choose conditions that are as favorable as possible: ideally, winds between 3—10 knots and calm, uncrowded waters. Always sail with an instructor or someone who knows how to windsurf well, and make sure that you have a clear idea of where the wind is coming from as well as the currents operating in the area. Your aim is to sail in and out at approximately 90° to the wind and return easily to your starting point. The easiest wind directions in which to learn are onshore to cross-shore winds. Offshore winds are very dangerous and should be avoided at all times.

In most situations, beginners tend to drift downwind, so you should aim slightly upwind and find a reference on the land before you start. When you are on the water, you can keep a regular check on the mark and see how far you have travelled. Remember, too, that currents and tides can carry, so be aware of your position at all times.

MANY WINDSURFING SCHOOLS USE DRY-LAND SIMULATORS TO EXPLAIN BASICS SUCH AS BODY AND FEET POSITION.

Safety and self-rescue

Although windsurfing is essentially a safe sport, it is always a good idea to remember that you are entering a potentially hazardous environment. It is wise to act sensibly and be well informed of potential hazards before you enter the water. It is imperative for all windsurfers to be aware of potential dangers and to know at least some of the self-rescue techniques. Just about every windsurfer will, at some time in their sailing career, regardless of their ability or experience, need to put these techniques into practice. It could be because the mast base has popped out of the board, or the wind has dropped to a level that makes sailing to land difficult or impossible; or there may be a more serious situation, such as severe change in the weather, or an injury.

The basic safety rules and techniques discussed on page 27 will minimize the chances of encountering problems, help you to deal with incidents that could spell danger and enable you to help someone else who might be in trouble.

WITH SMALLER, LIGHTER RIGS, CHILDREN AS YOUNG AS SIX YEARS OF AGE CAN ENJOY THE SPORT.

■ Learn to windsurf at a location with a permanently manned rescue boat and a fully qualified windsurfing instructor.

■ If you are not a confident swimmer, wear a buoyancy aid.

■ Wear the correct wetsuit for the climate. Even in hot climates, wind chill can suddenly develop into hypothermia, so make sure that you are well protected.

■ Never sail alone or if you are unsure of the location, weather conditions or your equipment. Find out as much as you can about tides, underwater hazards and any other local conditions.

■ Always sail within your own level of competence, or you risk getting yourself, and possibly others, into serious trouble.

■ Alert other water users or rescue services as soon as you or anyone else is in trouble.

■ If you are sailing in large, exposed waters, never sail in offshore winds. Despite this warning, many inexperienced sailors do go out in offshore winds. Don't!

■ Until you are an experienced windsurfer and have developed confidence on the water, stick to inland locations and protected waters. Being washed onto the banks of a lake rather than out to sea is a far safer way to be humbled by the sport.

■ Self rescue is easiest under conditions where there is little wind (see The butterfly on page 29). Where there is too much wind, however, you need to be far more cautious. These conditions may pose serious problems, so always head for the shore as soon as the wind starts to be too much for you.

■ Whenever you go windsurfing, always sail just a short distance out and then return to the shore. This way, you will be able to test if you are comfortable with your sail and whether you are able to

handle the conditions. You do not want to discover that you are out of your depth when you are way offshore — when it's too late to avoid trouble.

■ If the mast foot breaks or disconnects and you find yourself with a separated board and rig, always swim for the board first — and quickly! Due to its flotation, the board is easily blown away by the wind. Once you have the board, you should be safe. It is then easier to paddle and pick up the rig, which usually bobs on the surface of the water.

■ If you start to tire, head for the nearest shore. It doesn't have to be your departure point — just get to land quickly!

A WETSUIT, SUCH AS THIS WARM WEATHER SUIT, PROTECTS YOU FROM THE WIND AND SUN AND KEEPS YOU WARM IN WIND CHILL AND COLD WATER.

A WELL-FITTING BUOYANCY AID IS A MUST FOR WEAK SWIMMERS AND NOVICES — ESPECIALLY IN DEEP-WATER LOCATIONS.

THE INTERNATIONAL DISTRESS SIGNAL IS TO RAISE AND LOWER YOUR ARMS ABOVE YOUR HEAD TO ATTRACT ATTENTION TO THE FACT THAT YOU ARE EXPERIENCING DIFFICULTY IN THE WATER.

In distress

Once you realize that you are having difficulties in the water, or something has broken, act quickly or you may find yourself in serious trouble. Attract the attention of another windsurfer or water user. They may be able to assist in your immediate situation or at least alert a rescue team.

If there is no one within earshot, you will have to attract attention to yourself. The International Distress Signal is to continuously raise and lower both arms with clenched fists above your head. Many life jackets have 'Dayglo' flags and whistles, and these are very good ways of attracting attention to your situation.

The International Distress Signal works well at close distances, but a windsurfer on a board in the middle of a huge body of water may appear very small to onlookers. If you are in bright sunlight, try to catch the light on your watch and direct it towards other people.

Emergency de-rigging

Should either the conditions or equipment fail you, you will need to paddle back to the shore, and this means de-rigging. The first priority is to detach the rig from the board and then dismantle the rig. It is best to leave the mast base and extension in the board, as they don't float very well and you may lose them. Then disconnect the boom, place it across the board, and tie the uphaul to the extension to avoid losing it. While sitting on the board, un-sleeve the sail and roll it up as tightly as possible. Place the sail and mast on the deck and lie on top of it to keep it all in place. Then start to paddle to the shore. In rough seas it can be very difficult to de-rig and keep everything on board, in which case you should ditch the rig and paddle the board alone — but only if you are certain that you can make it back to shore. If not, leave the rig attached — it acts as an anchor, slows your rate of drift and is also the most visible item to rescue services.

IF IT IS IMPOSSIBLE TO WINDSURF BACK TO SHORE, DISMANTLING THE RIG WILL MAKE IT EASIER TO PADDLE THE BOARD OR HAUL EVERYTHING INTO A RESCUE BOAT.

Emergency measures
Help!
If you are out with experienced windsurfers, it is possible to slot one rig inside another rig. The rigless board can either be towed or paddled. This is quite an advanced technique and is usually only carried out by advanced sailors and experienced instructors.

The butterfly
If the wind dies, it is possible to lie the rig down across the back of the board and paddle back to shore.

IN VERY LIGHT WINDS, OR IF YOU ARE COMPLETELY 'BECALMED', IT IS POSSIBLE TO DISCONNECT THE RIG, LIE THROUGH IT ON THE BOARD AND PADDLE TO SHORE.

A MORE EXPERIENCED SAILOR MAY BE ABLE TO HELP BY SLOTTING YOUR RIG INTO THE ONE ON HIS BOARD, LEAVING YOU FREE TO PADDLE YOUR OWN BOARD BACK TO SHORE.

Sailing without a fin
A board will spin round in circles without a fin, so if the fin breaks you will find the board very difficult to sail. It is possible to sail short distances by tipping the board slightly on its side. Providing you don't sail too fast, this could be enough to help you get back to shore.

Towing
A rescue boat is the best way to return to land, but if for some reason one has not been alerted, another board can also get you back to shore. The best way to tow someone else is not from behind, but upwind and alongside the board that is being sailed.

EVEN IF THERE IS NO RESCUE BOAT, IT IS POSSIBLE FOR A WINDSURFER TO TOW ANOTHER WINDSURFER TO SAFETY. THIS MAY BE DIFFICULT IN ROUGH CONDITIONS, BUT IT HAS SAVED MANY A SAILOR.

Your first time on the water

Now that you're prepared, it's time to go windsurfing! Spend time familiarising yourself with the board. In the shallows, stand up on it, walk around on it, get a good idea of how the board responds to your body weight.

Uphauling

It's always worth getting wet early on in the game; it relaxes you and stops you trying to stay dry once you are up and going. Experiment fully before you mount the board and uphaul the rig.

STEP 1 WITH THE BOARD FACING SIDEWAYS INTO THE WIND AND THE RIG DOWNWIND OF THE BOARD, FACE THE BOARD WITH YOUR HANDS EACH SIDE OF THE MAST. SPRING UP ONTO THE BOARD, KEEPING YOUR WEIGHT IN THE CENTRE. ONCE STABLE, CROUCH AND FACE THE SAIL, WHICH SHOULD STILL BE LYING DOWNWIND. TAKE HOLD OF THE UPHAUL WITH THE HAND NEAREST TO THE BOARD'S FRONT. THIS PROVIDES STABILITY.

STEP 2 WITH THE UPHAUL NOW IN BOTH HANDS AND YOUR FEET ABOUT SHOULDER-WIDTH APART — AND ON EACH SIDE OF THE MAST BASE — YOU CAN START TO PULL THE SAIL UP TOWARDS YOU. DO NOT, HOWEVER, TRY TO DO THIS WITH YOUR ARM MUSCLES; RATHER LEAN BACK WITH YOUR BOTTOM TUCKED IN AND USE THE POWER IN YOUR LEGS AND YOUR BODY WEIGHT RATHER THAN FROM YOUR LOWER BACK AND ARMS.

STEP 3 AS THE SAIL STARTS TO LIFT OUT OF THE WATER, START TO STAND. KEEP YOUR BACK STRAIGHT, HEAD UP, AND PUSH WITH YOUR THIGHS, RATHER THAN YOUR LOWER BACK OR ARMS. IT HELPS IF YOU PULL THE RIG SLIGHTLY TOWARDS THE NOSE (OR TAIL, DEPENDING ON WHICH WAY THE RIG IS FACING), SLIDING THE RIG CLEAR RATHER THAN JERKING IT STRAIGHT OUT OF THE WATER. BY SLIDING THE MAST FORWARD AND UP, THE SAIL CUTS THROUGH THE WATER AND INTO THE WIND EASIER.

STEP 4 WITH THE RIG CLEAR OF THE WATER, THE WEIGHT IN THE RIG REDUCES, SO STOP LEANING BACK. CREATE A BALANCE, WITH THE RIG FORMING ONE SIDE OF A 'V' AND YOUR BODY THE OTHER. FEET SHOULD BE ACROSS THE CENTRE LINE, WITH HEELS JUST ON THE BOARD'S WIND-WARD SIDE. THE RIG SHOULD BE CLEAR, BUT NOT VERTICAL. YOU NEED DISTANCE BETWEEN YOUR BODY AND THE RIG AND THE BOARD SHOULD BE 90° TO THE WIND, WITH THE BOOM END CLEAR OF THE WATER.

BAD TECHNIQUE: THE BOTTOM IS OUT, THE HEAD IS DOWN AND THE BACK IS BENT. THIS PUTS UNNECESSARY STRAIN ON THE BACK.

Uphauling from a difficult position

The perfect uphaul situation is when the board is at 90° to the wind and the sail is lying downwind of the board, but the effects of wind and water mean that this is not always possible. Should the rig fall on the wrong side of the board, or the wind catches the sail and spins the board, you need to reposition yourself into the 'secure position' quickly.

STEP 1 THE WIND IS BLOWING OVER THE RIG, FORCING IT DOWN INTO THE WATER AND THE BOARD IS FACING THE WRONG DIRECTION, SO THERE IS NO POINT IN TRYING TO GO THROUGH THE WHOLE UPHAUL. ORIENTATE THE BOARD AND RIG TO MINIMIZE THE WEIGHT IN THE SAIL WELL BEFORE TRYING TO UPHAUL FULLY.

STEP 2 LEAN BACK JUST ENOUGH TO RAISE THE RIG SLIGHTLY AND ELEVATE THE LUFF, BUT DON'T RAISE THE RIG ENTIRELY OUT OF THE WATER. ASSERT PRESSURE VIA YOUR BACK FOOT BY PUTTING YOUR WEIGHT ON THE BACK LEG AND TRYING TO PUSH THE TAIL AWAY. THEN WAIT! WITH THE WIND BLOWING ONTO THE SAIL, THE BOARD WILL START TO SPIN. DON'T UPHAUL YET – EVEN IF THE SAIL STARTS TO LIFT. KEEP THE RIG TOWARDS THE BACK OF THE BOARD TO HELP THE BOARD TURN, KEEPING THE FRONT LEG SLIGHTLY BENT AND YOUR BACK LEG STRAIGHT.

STEP 3 YOU WILL KNOW WHEN YOU ARE IN A GOOD STARTING POSITION BECAUSE THE RIG WILL FEEL LIGHTER. DON'T WORRY IF THE BOARD GOES VIRTUALLY RIGHT ROUND INTO WIND; THIS WILL BE CORRECTED AS THE SAIL IS RAISED. WITH THE BOARD FACING MORE INTO THE WIND, THE RIG WILL LIFT OUT OF THE WATER FAR MORE EASILY. AS SOON AS THE RIG STARTS TO LIFT OUT OF THE WATER, START TO DISTRIBUTE YOUR WEIGHT MORE EVENLY ON BOTH FEET. NEVER SIMPLY PULL THE RIG UP OUT OF THE WATER.

STEP 1 CONCENTRATE ON HOLDING A STABLE BODY POSITION RATHER THAN RUSHING FOR THE RIG. IF THE BOARD REFUSES TO STAY AT 90° TO THE WIND OR THE SAIL WHEN THE RIG IS CLEAR OF THE WATER, YOU ARE EITHER LEANING THE RIG TOO FAR TO THE FRONT OR THE BACK OF THE BOARD. TO MAKE THE NOSE TURN AWAY FROM THE WIND, SWING THE RIG TOWARDS THE NOSE; TO MAKE THE NOSE FACE INTO THE WIND, SWING THE RIG TOWARDS THE TAIL. ALWAYS KEEP THE BODY FACING THE SAIL AND THE FEET ON EACH SIDE OF THE MAST.

STEP 2 PLACE YOUR FRONT HAND ON THE BOOM SO THAT IT IS NEAR THE MAST. MAKE SURE THAT YOU HAVE YOUR FRONT FOOT POSITIONED ALONGSIDE THE MAST BASE AND POINT IT FORWARD UP THE LENGTH OF THE BOARD (THE 'FRONT' HAND AND FOOT — A TERM FAMILIAR TO MOST SEASONED WINDSURFERS — ARE THOSE POSITIONED NEAREST THE FRONT OF THE BOARD). THE BOARD SHOULD BE AT 90° TO THE WIND, WITH THE RIG FACING DEAD DOWNWIND OF THE BOARD. DO NOT RUSH THIS STAGE, AND TRY NOT TO TENSE UP.

STEP 3 WITH THE FRONT HAND, DRAW THE RIG ACROSS YOUR BODY AND TOWARDS THE BOARD'S NOSE. THE RIG SHOULD BE CLEAR OF YOUR CHEST AND PULLED FAR ENOUGH ACROSS THAT YOU CAN SEE THE MAST IN LINE WITH THE BOARD'S NOSE. YOUR BACK HAND IS NOW WELL PLACED TO HOLD THE BOOM. PULLING THE RIG ACROSS YOUR BODY WILL STOP YOU BENDING AT THE WAIST AND REACHING ACROSS THE BOARD TO GRAB THE BOOM. BE ASSERTIVE WITH THE RIG AND FIRM WITH THE FRONT ARM TO KEEP THE RIG UPRIGHT.

STEP 4 ONCE YOUR BACK HAND IS ON THE BOOM, 'SHEET THE SAIL IN' BY PULLING ON THE BACK HAND AND EXTENDING AND PULLING YOUR REAR SHOULDER AWAY FROM THE RIG. THIS ACTION WILL SERVE TO FILL THE SAIL WITH WIND AND THE BOARD WILL THEN START TO MOVE FORWARD WITH THE WIND.

TRY TO RELAX YOUR BODY AND SIMPLY LEAN GENTLY BACK AGAINST THE PULL OF THE SAIL. ALWAYS TRY TO KEEP A GOOD DISTANCE BETWEEN YOUR HEAD AND THE RIG.

Getting underway

A successful start depends almost entirely on body position. Your body is facing forward, your hands are shoulder-width apart on the boom, front arm straight, and back arm slightly bent to sheet the sail in and out. The body is facing forward with the head up and hips in. The rig is almost upright, creating a 'V' between the sailor and the mast and mast base. From this position, it is easier to feel the wind in the sail and balance on the board. Generally, in very light winds, the mast is held leeward of the board's centerline and, as the wind increases, the mast becomes more upright. In stronger winds, the rig is pulled slightly to windward of the centerline as the sailor hangs off the boom.

THE CORRECT STANCE OF THE BODY DEMANDS THAT THE HEAD IS LOOKING FORWARD AND THE RIG IS UPRIGHT, SO THAT THE WINDSURFER AND THE MAST CREATE THE PREFERRED 'V' POSITION.

Controlling the power

The power in the rig is controlled by how much the boom is 'sheeted in and out' — moving the clew towards and away from the wind. Imagine that the rig is a door. If the door is open and lying downwind like a flag, it delivers no power. If the door is closed — in other words, the boom is pulled closer to the board — it exposes the sail to the wind and increases the power and drive.

When sailing, the front hand holds the mast upright, while the back hand acts as the throttle, trimming the position of the boom to deliver the power. The board sails more smoothly and is more comfortable when underway, so the sail should be sheeted in sufficiently to maintain a comfortable speed. If you want to slow down or if the wind suddenly gusts and the power is too much, the back hand and boom is eased out slightly (15–60cm/6–24 inches is usually enough to lose some excess power).

When the sail is sheeted in and exposed to the wind, don't be afraid to resist the pull by leaning the shoulders out and back towards the wind and away from the rig — especially the rear shoulder, which extends away from the rig and towards the wind to counteract the pull in the sail. Dropping the body lower and outward will help.

Holding the rig

To gain and control extra power in the rig, both hands can move further down the boom towards the clew. This makes it easier to handle any extra pull in the sail and makes it easier to keep the rig sheeted in, which is vital to your progress in windsurfing. The 'sheeting in' action is pretty much continuous as you resist the pull in the sail. On the water, the back arm is usually bent slightly more than the front arm to ensure the rig is sheeted in and pulling you forward.

You will eventually need to learn to accelerate and control your board under greater speed and stronger wind conditions (see Mastering the Technique on page 34) but, for now, rather choose a sail you can handle and practice sheeting in with the back hand situated well down the boom.

Mastering the Technique

Like a dinghy or a yacht, a windsurfer can sail at various angles to the wind. But where the boat's buoyancy is forgiving and the rig is fixed, a windsurfer rig needs to be constantly balanced and trimmed when changing course. Although most people simply sail in and out on the same course with little change, windsurfing enthusiasts use different 'points of sailing' each time they go out, requiring specific stances to accommodate any change of direction.

When you are on the water, your stance changes gradually as the board alters course. In time it becomes a natural feeling, but remember that, in mastering technique, you will need to appreciate the conditions in which you are sailing and to understand the forces of wind and water at play on your rig while it is in the water (see How a sail works on page 39).

Steering the board

In order to maneuver yourself skillfully across the water, you need to understand the simple dynamics of your board. The board responds to where you are standing on it, but it also reacts to where the rig is positioned. If you want to alter the board's course, you have to change the rig's alignment to the board. To do this, you need to tilt the rig backwards or forwards along the centerline of the board. In reality, steering is only a matter of making slight adjustments to the rig, not bold movements. As you improve, these movements become quite subtle, so take time to experiment with your board. You will find that you can change the board's speed by actually changing the direction of travel. Heading away from the wind speeds the board up. Sailing towards the wind slows it down.

above ALL BOARDS CAN BE TURNED TIGHTLY AND ACCURATELY WHEN BOTH BODY AND RIG ARE POSITIONED CORRECTLY.

opposite WHEN SAILING IN A STRAIGHT LINE, IT IS VITAL TO BE ABLE TO CHANGE COURSE TO CONTROL THE BOARD'S SPEED AND DIRECTION.

BEARING OR TURNING AWAY FROM THE WIND.

LUFFING UP OR TURNING TOWARDS THE WIND.

Bearing away

Turning or bearing away from the wind increases the volume of wind in the sail, and thus increases the power. This will help you to get the board going again if you have sailed too far into the wind, or to increase your speed slightly if the board has slowed down while sailing upwind. Tilting the rig towards the nose of the board will turn it 'off the wind' or 'bear away'.

While maintaining a stable position, extend your front hand forward towards the nose, and sheet in with the back hand — much like turning a set of raised handlebars. You should be standing just windward of the centerline and sink onto the back foot to stop being pulled forward by the increased pull of the rig. When you have turned the board onto your desired course, bring the rig back to a more upright position and resume normal sailing.

Luffing up

Luffing up, or turning the board towards the wind, causes the sail to lose power and effectively slows you down. Think of luffing up as your brake — very useful if the board starts to go too fast. Also known as heading upwind, luffing up is achieved by leaning the rig back towards the tail along the centerline and placing additional weight on the back foot to help the board move. Luffing up is much easier than bearing away from the wind — in fact, so much so that it is often done unintentionally while sailing. A windsurfer cannot sail closer than approximately 45° to the wind, so luffing up is only a temporary action to establish a new course. Otherwise, you will simply continue to head into the wind and will come to a stop. So, once the board has changed a few degrees, it is important to resume a normal sailing position.

IF THE BOARD IS LUFFING TOO MUCH, YOU NEED TO GAIN CONTROL OVER THE RIG. SHIFT YOUR BACK HAND RIGHT DOWN THE BOOM, ALMOST AS FAR AS YOU CAN REACH. FROM THIS POSITION, EXTEND THE FRONT ARM AND TILT THE RIG FORWARD TOWARDS THE NOSE.

SOMETIMES THE BOARD IS RELUCTANT TO TURN, SO YOU NEED TO ACCENTUATE EVERYTHING FROM A LOW POSITION. DROPPING LOWER NOT ONLY MAKES YOU MORE STABLE AND LESS LIKELY TO BE PULLED FORWARD BY THE RIG'S POWER, BUT ALSO ENABLES YOU TO PUSH THROUGH THE FRONT FOOT, WHICH IS BEST PLACED RIGHT UP NEXT AND JUST TO WINDWARD OF THE MAST BASE. PUSHING HARD THROUGH THE TOES HELPS FORCE THE BOARD AWAY. THE SHEETING IN ACTION AND FORWARD RAKE TWISTS THE RIG, FILLS IT WITH MORE WIND AND MOVES THE CENTER OF EFFORT IN THE SAIL TOWARDS THE NOSE. THIS IMMEDIATELY HELPS TURN THE NOSE AWAY FROM THE WIND. AS THE RIG MOVES FORWARD, DO NOT GO WITH IT. ONCE THE BOARD IS ON ITS NEW COURSE YOU CAN RESUME A MORE COMFORTABLE STANCE WITH THE RIG IN A MORE UPRIGHT POSITION.

Preventing too much luffing

Heading too far into the wind is a common — and frustrating — mistake, and usually slows the board down quite dramatically. Inevitably, the sailor will find it very difficult to avoid being 'back winded'. If allowed to take its own course, a board will usually head into the wind, so knowing how to detect and deal with the board's tendency to luff will enable you to prevent it.

■ The closer the mast track is to the dagger board, the more pivotal the board will be and the more likely it will be to turn into the wind. If you have a sliding or adjustable track, keep the mast base in the middle position; if you continue luffing, try moving it slightly forward.

■ When using a dagger board, the chances of luffing are heightened by any increase in wind. If you find yourself in gusty winds above Force 3, retracting the dagger board will drastically reduce the luffing tendency.

A common predicament

A typical luffing situation is when the board is pointing almost directly into the wind. This, of course, leaves you with very little room to control the rig as the boom comes in towards you. At this point, if the rig is simply sheeted in, the board will head further into the wind. It is not long, then, until you are inevitably back winded and drop into windward.

Where to stand

Your position on the board will have a considerable effect on the board's trim. There is no precise position, but you will soon begin to sense when the board is poorly trimmed and will learn — through trial and error — how to gain a secure footing on a stable board.

When you learn to uphaul and get going, have both feet balanced directly across the centerline, with one foot either side of the mast base. This position is ideal for raising and balancing the rig before you get going, but once the board starts to move it is important to re-establish a secure footing to resist the rig.

POSITIONING THE FEET ACROSS THE BOARD WITH ONE FOOT EITHER SIDE OF THE CENTERLINE ACCENTUATES THE TILTING ACTION AS THE WEIGHT NATURALLY SHIFTS BETWEEN EACH FOOT WHEN THE BOARD RESPONDS TO THE WATER.

WITH THE FEET ACROSS THE BOARD, THE WEIGHT TENDS TO SHIFT FROM TOE TO HEEL, ACCENTUATING THE BOARD'S NATURAL TILT FROM SIDE TO SIDE. THIS CAN BE UNSETTLING AND TILTS THE SAILOR ONTO THE TOES AND TOWARDS THE SAIL IF A GUST HITS, OR ONTO THE HEELS AND AWAY FROM THE SAIL IF THERE IS A LULL IN THE WIND.

Controlling pitch and tilt

Adopt a simple foot stance with the front foot pointing forward and the heel of the back foot windward. The forward-facing front foot helps push the board flat and opens up the hips slightly, positioning the body to lean outboard and back if the board accelerates. The back foot reduces tilt and is poised to step back to resist a gust. Experiment on your footwork. A jaunt up and down the board will indicate 'no-go' areas, and will give you the feel of how a board responds to pressure.

Pitch

Despite the length of a long board, it is important to keep it flat on all planes. See-sawing will not assist in either control or comfort. When the board is travelling slowly, you may decide to place your feet up at the mast foot. As the board accelerates, your body weight should be shifted into a rearward position to resist the power in the sail and prevent the nose from ploughing. Otherwise, the board will stall and you will be pulled forward by the rig.

TO CONTROL PITCH AND TILT, PLACE THE FRONT FOOT JUST TO WIND-WARD, POINTING FORWARD AND ALONGSIDE THE MAST BASE. THE BACK FOOT SHOULD LIE ACROSS THE CENTERLINE WITH THE HEEL EDGING ONTO THE WINDWARD SIDE.

Moving forward

When the wind makes contact with a sail, the air flow separates and passes each side of the sail. On the leeward side, air flow accelerates over the curve of the sail, resulting in a reduction in air pressure. On the windward side, there is a high pressure area that pushes towards the low pressure, thus creating drive and power in the sail. The drive is turned into forward motion by the shape of the sail, which is sucked forward due to the difference in pressure on the two sides.

This drive and power from the sail is transferred down into the board through the mast base. The underside of the board, fin and dagger board create lateral resistance and prevent the board from slipping sideways, and so it sails forwards.

Using body weight

In strong winds, windsurfers learn to use their body to counteract the force of wind in the sail. The extra pull of the sail can be tiring over long periods so, to combat fatigue and help control power, proficient windsurfers use a harness. Hooked into a fixed line off the boom, it is possible to control the pull of the sail by leaning back and down.

Center of effort

Every sail has a 'center of effort' (CE), which is where the power of the sail is concentrated. This is usually close to the center of the sail and at about head height. The CE is balanced against the board's 'center of lateral resistance' (CLR), about in the center of the board and from where the board pivots. In light winds, steering is accomplished by leaning the rig forward so that the CE in the sail is forward of the CLR in the board. This pushes the nose away from the wind. Leaning the rig back — so that the CE is behind the CLR — has the opposite effect and pushes the tail away from the wind, turning the nose towards the wind. This can be done in minimal or exaggerated movements, depending on how much you need or want to turn the board.

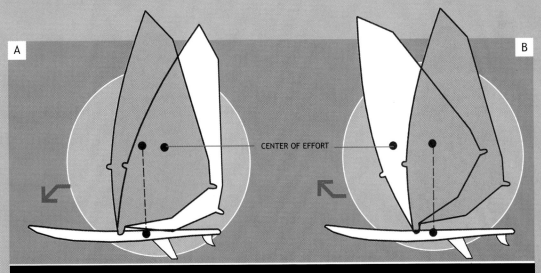

CENTER OF EFFORT

A IF THE RIG IS RAKED TOWARDS THE TAIL, THE CENTER OF EFFORT MOVES BACKWARDS AND WILL ENCOURAGE THE BOARD TO TURN TOWARDS THE WIND.

B WHEN THE RIG IS MOVED TOWARDS THE NOSE, THE CENTER OF EFFORT MOVES FORWARD AND HELPS TURN THE BOARD AWAY FROM THE WIND.

Turning round

Once you are able to get on the board and sail off, you will need to learn how to turn around on the water. The board can be turned either into or away from the wind and you should practice this during your first sessions on the board. It is important to build your confidence in turning, so try it out in the safety of the shallows rather than on the horizon.

The most basic method of turning a board round — where the rig is held using the uphaul rope — is a vital starting point, but is used largely to align the board in the direction of travel before getting going. Tacking (see page 46) and jibing (see page 50) will help you turn the board while you are underway and holding the boom.

Turning maneuvers

There are basically two methods of turning around: tacking, where the rig passes over the back of the board, and jibing, where the rig passes over the front

ALL WINDSURFERS NEED TO BE ABLE TO TURN. WITH EXPERIENCE, THIS BECOMES A FAST AND EXHILARATING MANEUVER, BUT YOU NEED TO MASTER THE BASICS BEFORE YOU CAN TURN AT HIGH SPEEDS.

of the board. The sole purpose of turning the board is to be able to return from where you left by aligning the board onto your chosen course. The simplest methods of turning the board are the 'rope tack' and 'rope jibe', and the technique is the same. Whether you choose to turn into or away from the wind will depend on which way you wish to head and what obstacles you may wish to avoid.

From a normal starting position — if you want to turn the board 180° and sail back the opposite way — start by releasing the back hand and letting the rig fly downwind. Holding the mast (or uphaul) with both hands, stand with your feet on either side of the mast base, and then swing the rig towards the nose (if jibing) or tail (if tacking), keeping the clew clear of the water at all times.

As you swing the rig, it will eventually lie directly down the board and move across it. The rig needs to be handled assertively — this 'swinging' action is best likened to a two-handed, slow baseball bat swing. Hold the rig out in front of you, keep a firm grip on the rope and do not rush it. Once the rig has crossed over the tail (tacking) or nose (jibing), continue to turn the board until it is aligned 90° to the wind and is ready on the new tack to sail again.

Starting off in the new direction follows precisely the same procedure as you completed before, except the opposite hand will be your front hand. It is always the front hand that is on the mast (or boom near the mast) when you start off.

Turning 180°

When turning the board 180° away from the wind, it is vital that you move your feet as you swing the rig around. Throughout the entire maneuver, you should have your legs more or less straddling the mast, with your heels to windward of the base, your back to the wind and your body facing the mast.

To maintain a positive, solid position, take lots of little, shuffling steps as the board goes round. In fact, it is important that you keep moving as the rig moves across the back of the board — otherwise you will be knocked off.

STEP 1 SHEET THE SAIL OUT. WHEN THE BOARD HAS SLOWED DOWN, TRANSFER BOTH HANDS TO THE MAST (OR UPHAUL). IT IS AT THIS POINT THAT YOU SHOULD START TO SWING THE RIG SO THAT IT POINTS TOWARDS THE NOSE OF THE BOARD.

STEP 2 WITH A SWINGING ACTION, DROP THE RIG TOWARDS THE NOSE AND INTO THE WIND. THE KNEES SHOULD BE SLIGHTLY BENT FOR STABILITY AND TO STOP BREAKING AT THE WAIST. THE BODY BALANCES AGAINST THE WEIGHT OF THE RIG.

STEP 3 AS THE BOARD TURNS FURTHER, TAKE SMALL STEPS TO KEEP THE BODY FACING THE MAST. AS THE RIG SWINGS ACROSS THE BOARD, KEEP ONE FOOT EACH SIDE OF THE MAST FOOT AND THE HEELS TO WINDWARD OF THE CENTERLINE.

STEP 4 WHILE MAINTAINING THE SWING, AND USING YOUR FEET IN SUCH A WAY THAT THEY 'ENCOURAGE' THE BOARD TO TURN, PIVOT THE BOARD AROUND UNTIL YOU ARE READY ON THE OTHER TACK. YOU HAVE NOW SUCCESSFULLY TURNED THE BOARD.

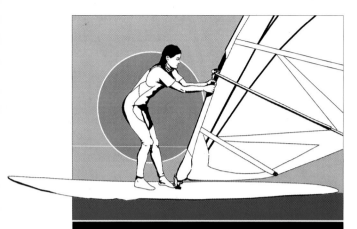

IN THE ROPE TACK, LIKE THE ROPE GYBE, THE RIG IS SWUNG ACROSS THE BOARD TO MAKE IT TURN. DURING THE ROPE TACK, THE BACK OF THE BOOM PASSES OVER THE TAIL OF THE BOARD.

THERE ARE MANY REASONS WHY YOU COULD FALL OR BE KNOCKED OFF YOUR BOARD; IT HAPPENS TO EVERYONE. AVOID INJURY AND DAMAGE TO YOUR EQUIPMENT BY TRYING NOT TO LAND ON THE BOARD OR SAIL.

The rope tack

The rope tack is the opposite of the rope jibe (see page 41) and the rig is swung across the tail of the board. This method often feels more stable and is particularly useful if you are trying to make your way back upwind after drifting downwind.

Moving your feet

It is quite common that windsurfers do not move their feet quickly enough as the board pivots round. Your feet should shuffle round in time with the rig's movement. If they do not, you will run the risk of being knocked off by the hard mast. The way out of this is to always move the feet.

Points to remember

■ The rig The closer you sail to the wind, the more the rig is sheeted in. This means that the clew is closer to the tail of the board. As you turn away from the wind, with the rig more to the front of your body, the more the rig is sheeted out.

■ Body and feet The closer you sail to the wind, the more the body and feet face across the board. As you turn away from the wind, the body and feet point forward and up the board.

Dagger boards

Dagger boards provide lateral resistance and make the board more manoeuvrable and sensitive to turning. Whenever sailing in light winds — especially when heading upwind — it is best to have the dagger board right down. As you become accustomed to stronger breezes and higher speed the dagger board can be fully retracted. There is never a time when the dagger board is situated halfway between the two points.

Terms to remember

■ Blasting Sailing in and out on a beam reach. In other words, leave the shore, go out, turn around, and sail back to your departure point.

■ Sailing pretty tight Sailing quite close to or into the wind. This usually refers to a situation in which the dagger board is down and the windsurfer is trying to move upwind — possibly back to the shore after having drifted downwind.

■ Sailing quite broad Sailing away from the wind on a broad reach (see page 43), usually with the dagger board up. This is when the board travels fastest.

Sailing and steering

1. Sailing upwind This means you are heading towards the wind at 45°, blowing onto your front shoulder. The rig should be raked back with the boom sheeted in, bringing the clew towards the tail. Your body faces across the board and the feet push sideways, with the heels windward of the centerline. To stop the board slipping sideways, the dagger board would be right down.

2. Close reaching The board is turned off the wind, at 60–45° from true wind direction, blowing onto the back of your leading shoulder. The rig is more sheeted out, with the mast more upright than the upwind position. The front foot starts to face forward to keep the board from turning too far into the wind.

3. Beam reaching The board is 90° to the wind, with the mast upright, but the boom still sheeted in. With the wind blowing across your back, lean out far and balance against the sail, your body hanging over the side. The front foot still faces forward, with hips and shoulders focused across the board. If the board goes fast or keeps heading into the wind, retract the dagger board.

4. Broad reaching The wind blows over your rear shoulder and down the board. You are sailing about 120° from true wind direction — feet, hips and shoulders open up and face down the board. To lean back and resist the wind's force, lean towards the tail, rather than outboard. The rig is more sheeted out and the mast is pulled upright as the board is blown along. As the board moves faster, edge slightly further back on the board to stop the nose diving. This point of sailing is also easier if the dagger board is retracted.

5. Running The wind blows down the board, the rig is sheeted out and at 90° to the board, obscuring your view of the nose. The power from the rig is now focused up and down, rather than from the side of the board. To counter the rig's pull, the body should focus directly down the board. Note how both feet face towards the front and stand on either side of the centerline to control the board's tilt. Your feet will move back and forth to balance the board's pitch. In light winds and choppy water, sailing directly downwind can feel quite wobbly. Running is the most unstable point of sailing.

Developing your stance

Windsurfing can be so much easier if you establish a balanced, controlled and relaxed stance, especially as you progress towards more testing conditions.

As with any sport, experts make it look easy because they do not 'fight' against their equipment — they work in harmony with it to achieve the desired result. Why pull when you can just hang? Why push when you can simply lean? Same end result, but half the effort.

Getting it right

■ HANDS Your hands have a relaxed grip and are about shoulder-width apart.
■ SHOULDERS Your shoulders should be leaning back and your arms relaxed.
■ HEAD You are facing outboard, looking forward.
■ HIPS Your hips are raised upwards.
■ FEET Your feet are positioned behind the mast, to windward of the centerline, with your front foot angled slightly forward.

RELAXED GRIP WITH HANDS SHOULDER-WIDTH APART

HEAD OUTBOARD AND LOOKING FORWARD

ARMS RELAXED AND SHOULDERS BACK

HIPS RAISED

FEET BEHIND THE MAST, TO WINDWARD OF THE CENTRELINE, WITH FRONT FOOT ANGLED SLIGHTLY FORWARD

WITH PRACTICE, YOU WILL DEVELOP A STANCE THAT WILL MAKE THE RIG SEEM LIGHTER, AND MORE STABLE, MANOEUVRABLE AND CONTROLLABLE.

HEAD FACING THE SAIL

HANDS TOO WIDE APART

HIPS STICKING OUT

SHOULDERS INBOARD

FEET TOO WIDE APART AND FACING DIRECTLY ACROSS THE BOARD

THIS TYPICAL BEGINNER'S STANCE MAKES THE RIG HEAVY, SUSCEPTIBLE TO GUSTS, AND THE BOARD UNSTABLE AND DIFFICULT TO TURN.

Hands

Your hands are a direct link to the rig and you need to be sensitive to changes in rig position and wind direction. To save energy and enable a relaxed grip, hold the boom using your hands as 'hooks' rather than claws. Your fist should be slightly open, with the wrist lower than boom level. This reduces the possibility of blisters and the workload on the forearms.

Grip

It is universally accepted that an overhand grip on the back hand is more comfortable and effective. The choice for the front hand is less well defined and you will see sailors happily using an underhand grip. However, during your initiation to the sport, an underhand grip is probably best avoided as it can create a tendency to bend the front arm and will bring your upper body too close to the rig. By using the overhand grip, the front arm is more inclined to straighten and relax.

A wide 'gorilla-style' grip on the boom brings the body in close and reduces your ability to counterbalance the pull of the rig should a gust hit. Too narrow a grip makes it difficult to hold onto the rig when the board changes direction or suddenly increases in speed.

The ideal position is for your hands to be roughly shoulder-width apart. To cope with variation in wind direction and speed, it is crucial to be prepared to move the hands along the boom (the stronger the wind, the more rearward the grip). Avoid a fixed-position death grip, move both hands up and down the boom to find a comfortable balance point – thus allowing you to sheet in – lean out and resist the power in the sail.

A relaxed, straight-arm stance is the only way to be comfortable for long periods. Any considerable bending of the arms will tire you out quickly and means you are using muscle rather than technique to control the rig.

Arms

It's a fallacy that to sheet in you bend your arms in isolation. The point is to distance yourself from the rig and use body weight rather than muscle to counteract the rig's power. The action of leaning back, dropping and extending the rear shoulder outboard, sheets the sail

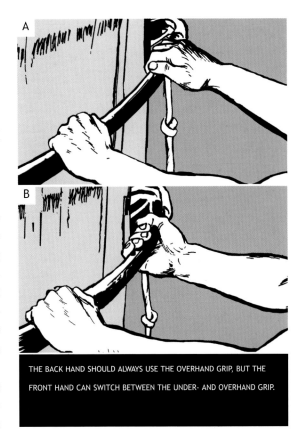

THE BACK HAND SHOULD ALWAYS USE THE OVERHAND GRIP, BUT THE FRONT HAND CAN SWITCH BETWEEN THE UNDER- AND OVERHAND GRIP.

in. In reality, the back arm does actually bend slightly during this process, but it is the outboard, upper body and rear shoulder that does most of the work.

Hips

The hips are your center of ballast and are integral to your posture. The action of raising the hips encourages your shoulders to move outward and creates a straight body position to push the board forward. The hips drop when a strong gust hits and you need to lower the body weight quickly to counteract the rig's excessive pull.

Legs

Use the legs to push against the board and help extend the body away. If your legs are relatively straight then all the forces from the rig will be directed through the board, making it sail straighter and accelerate in gusts. Your front leg should be relaxed but straight, the back leg slightly bent to absorb the rig's power and allow the board to tilt and pitch to the water state.

Tacking

The basic 180° turn is an integral part of their wind-surfing. This is the most stable way to turn a board, plus it keeps you upwind during the process.

While large boards are quite stable to tack, it is worth working to improve and speed up your tacks. As you progress through the sport and sail in stronger winds and on smaller boards, you have less stabilty and, therefore, less time; speed and timing are essential.

The basic principle of a tack is to sail the board into the wind and, as the nose passes through the eye of the wind, the sailor steps around the mast onto the 'new' side of the board. In a 'tack' the boom and mast are used to keep the power in the sail during the entry and exit, making the whole turn much faster.

The approach

To make a controlled tack, first adopt a stable stance that encourages the board to sail effortlessly into the wind and, secondly, create a situation where the rig is raked back sufficiently to enable unhindered movement around the mast when the board is 'head to wind'. Unfortunately, impatience and nerves seem to take over during the early part of the transition, causing the inexperienced sailor to neglect the rig rake and move prematurely towards the mast base, effectively starting the tack action while still on a beam reach. This instantly reduces the turning capabilities of any board and also your stability, so use what you already know and sail the board into the wind for as long as possible. Then run through the approach sequence.

BY LEANING THE SAIL TOWARDS THE TAIL OF THE BOARD AND MOVING ROUND THE FRONT OF THE MAST, IT IS POSSIBLE TO TURN THE BOARD A COMPLETE 180° AND SAIL BACK IN THE DIRECTION FROM WHICH YOU CAME.

Initiation

Assuming you are already on an upwind course, without otherwise changing your body position, place your front hand on the mast, just below the boom. Later, when you might be wearing a harness, you would unhook before doing this. Lean the rig towards the back of the board, with the clew roughly along the centerline. Think of the rig as a metronome: this being the first swing.

Aim to rake the rig as far back as it will go without putting the clew into the water. As you do this, your weight should be on the back foot. Provided you have executed this correctly, the board will turn. If you remained in this position, the board would head into the wind and knock you off, so you need to prepare to move round the mast.

As the board heads upwind, place the front foot in front of the mast base. Ideally, this should happen in a smooth motion: lean the sail back, add weight to your back foot and step forward with the front foot. Your legs should be wide apart, with your back foot pushing the board's tail away from you. The more weight exerted through the back foot, and the greater the rig rake, the faster the board will turn.

After a few attempts, the board slows down the closer it gets to the true wind direction. Before it passes through the eye of the wind, slide the back foot slightly forward so that your feet are only shoulder-width apart, but still leaving the rig raked back. Think 'rig back, body forward'. Keeping the rig raked back maintains the turning momentum. Moving forward provides a balance point against the rig and prepares you for that final step forward before pivoting around the mast.

The step

When you are 'head to wind', the rig will go lighter and you will find it easy to pull the clew over the back of the board. Try to delay stepping right around the mast until the turning momentum takes the nose of the board right through the eye of the wind. This makes the timing of the step forward fairly crucial. Go too early and the board won't keep turning; leave it too late, and you can be 'back winded'. As the board comes up into the wind your front foot should be firmly in position, just in front and to windward of the mast base. It is vital to keep the rig raked back with a tight grip on the mast hand — you do not want to drop the rig now!

BEGIN THE TACKING MANEUVER BY POINTING YOUR BOARD INTO THE WIND AND THEN SAILING UPWIND.

PLACE THE FRONT HAND ON THE MAST AND START TO LEAN THE SAIL BACK TOWARDS THE TAIL.

The pivot

To avoid being blown off backwards when the board is head to wind, establish a stable body position by subtly sliding the front foot across the centerline of the board in front of the mast base.

This action starts to bring the body forward slightly, but the rig must stay back to create room for the pivot around the mast. Just as the nose starts to point onto the new tack, the rig often comes in towards the body and the foot of the sail will push against the shin. Now is the time to make the move around the reclined mast.

To simultaneously force the nose right through the wind and to move the body forward, spring off the back foot in one bold, assertive step. Once in front of the mast base, pivot on the ball of the front foot. During the split second where the body faces the tail, it is important not to bend at the waist under the weight from the raked rig. To prevent this, keep the knees slightly bent and the head up.

Hands and feet

During the step and pivot, the hand change should remain simple. So, with a firm grip on the mast with the front hand, release the back hand and place it on the new side of the boom (near the boom clamp for maximum leverage). The body is upright but the mast is still raked back and clear from the chest, creating space for the hand change. If you prefer, it is perfectly acceptable to place the 'new' front hand on the mast rather than the boom — although placing it on the boom minimizes the number of moves and provides a more secure grip. Use whichever is the easiest for you. Either way, once the new front hand has been established, it is time to release the 'old' front hand from the mast and swiftly continue the rest of the move.

Try not to hesitate. Think about getting the new front foot pointing forward by pivoting and twisting on the balls of the feet. Keep the body directly over the board and concentrate on forcing the rig forward, away from the chest.

AS THE RIG RAKES BACK YOU NEED TO STEP FORWARD ON THE BOARD, USING YOUR FRONT FOOT.

WHEN THE BOARD PASSES THROUGH THE EYE OF THE WIND, STEP FORWARD WITH THE BACK FOOT, KEEPING THE RIG AWAY FROM YOU.

TO EXIT THE TACK, MOVE THE MAST FORWARD AND STEP BACK WITH THE BODY.

ONCE ON THE NEW TACK, RESUME A NORMAL SAILING POSITION AND SAIL AWAY.

Sailing away

To complete the tack, you need to reverse the rig and body positions. Going into the tack, the rig is back and the body is forward.

After the pivot (see page 48), the rig is leant forward and the body drops back. The rig has now transferred from being raked back virtually over the tail, to leaning towards the nose, while the body has moved from a forward position near the mast base to right back towards the tail.

The action is this ...

■ The first step is to make sure that your front arm, strong and positive, throws the mast towards the nose, roughly along the centerline of the board.
■ At the same time, you need to make sure that the back foot steps well down the board.
■ The back hand reaches far down the boom, but does not sheet in hard yet.
■ Wait until the rig is completely forward and the body has dropped low — virtually below the boom via a bent back leg — then sheet in and sail away. The steps to get to this point simply demand some practice.

Think Number 7!

Adopt a stance that drives the board forward and allows the body to adjust easily to wind fluctuations. As you progress you will have more time to develop and notice minor differences in stance. As a beginner, work through the points on dry land while holding the rig to the wind. As you do this, think of holding a relaxed stance that resembles the number 7.

Jibing

Quite opposite to the tack, during a jibe the body stays in position and the rig is swung around the front of the board. Jibing, like tacking, turns the board 180°, but in the jibe the board is turned downwind.

This maneuver can be performed with the dagger board up or down, but if the dagger board is down the board will only turn by continued pressure on the outside (windward) rail. When the dagger board is up, the board will not turn as tightly, but it will be much easier to retain control and initiate the turn in marginal winds.

Dagger board

■ Down This tightens the turning circle but requires continued pressure on the outside rail. The move can be a little tricky in stronger winds as the board tends to tilt over quite easily.

■ Up This increases stability and control in strong winds and makes it easier to turn on a flat plane.

The entry

Before starting the jibe, bear the board away onto a broad reach. This means that you sail the first part of the turn to increase stability. To avoid being pulled forward by the surge of power in the rig that is characteristic of bearing away, drop your weight back and push hard through the toes of the front foot, which should be placed just to windward and slightly behind the mast base. To help the board to turn, the rig should be leaning forward towards the nose and along the centerline of the board (to do this, straighten the front arm and stay sheeted in with the back hand to keep power in the sail). If the sail sheets out, the sail will back wind and the mast will fall to windward or towards the tail.

As the board bears away your body should start to turn to face up the board; shuffle your feet until they are placed either side of the board and point towards the mast base, with your head and hips directly over the centerline. As the board bears away, take a few short steps back towards the tail. The further back you move, the tighter and quicker the board will turn. To keep power in the sail, keep the rig out in front of you.

STEP 1 TO START THE JIBE, BEAR THE BOARD AWAY.

STEP 2 AS THE BOARD BEARS AWAY, DROP LOW AND MOVE BACK.

STEP 3 TO ENCOURAGE THE BOARD TO TURN, LEAN THE RIG OUT OF THE TURN.

STEP 4 AS THE BOARD TURNS ONTO THE NEW TACK IT IS TIME TO FLIP THE RIG.

STEP 5 AS THE RIG BEGINS TO FLIP, PLACE THE 'NEW' FRONT HAND ONTO THE MAST.

STEP 6 TO SAIL AWAY, BRING THE MAST FORWARD AND SHEET IN WITH THE BACK HAND.

Turning

To turn the board you have to lean the rig forward and to windward. The more you lean it to windward (to the outside of the turning circle), the faster the board will pivot. To retain control, keep your back hand well sheeted in so that the boom is parallel with the body and the clew is at about head height. This can be made easier by simply using a wider grip on the boom. If the wind gusts, there can be quite a pull from the rig, so always keep the knees slightly bent and sit back onto an imaginary stool to stop being pulled forward and to encourage the board to turn.

To increase the turning speed and force the board away from the wind, apply slightly more pressure through the foot on the windward rail (the foot on the outside of the turn). This should feel rather like taking a corner on a road with an adverse camber; the body feels like it is falling out of the turn. As the rig is leaned out of the turn, counterbalance with the body to stop yourself from being pulled over by the rig. If you keep your feet firmly on either side of the board, facing forward and maintaining a low body position by bending the knees, the possibility of falling out of the turn is minimized. If you feel unbalanced at any time during the jibe, a shuffle of the feet should restore your body position. The more you can experiment with foot pressure and position, the quicker you will learn.

Keeping the board turning

You are trying to turn the board 180°, so do not flip the rig until the board is pointing out on to the new direction. Wait until you are facing the direction from which you came before completing the jibe.

To keep the board turning beyond the downwind point, continue leaning the mast to windward and out of the turn while maintaining pressure on the outside rail with your back foot. If the clew starts to pull forward it is a good indication that the board has passed the downwind stage and is now coming round onto the new tack. To allow the board to turn, ease out the back hand. There will be a surge of power, so drop the body weight by bending your knees and resist the pull in the sail. As the board comes round onto the new tack, keep the rig away from your body and step forward with the 'new' front foot. This brings the body forward into a more stable position and stops the tail from sinking.

AS YOU ADVANCE THROUGH THE SPORT IT IS POSSIBLE TO TURN THE BOARD AT SPEED, BUT THIS REQUIRES GOOD TIMING AND BALANCE.

The rig flip

Hold onto the rig until the board is pointing almost back the way it came, sailing 'clew first' for a few of seconds before actually flipping the rig. If the rig is released too early the mast will fall behind and towards the tail. As soon as the back hand is released, the aim is to place it on the mast (below the boom) or on the 'new' (or other) side of the boom, whichever you prefer. This change of the hands can be unsettling, so keep your body (and center of gravity) low, once again holding the rig away from you as a balance point. Be very solid on the feet and try to keep your head and hips over the board.

Because there is considerable power in the rig during the flip, it is vital that you have a firm grip with the new front hand. Your best chance of keeping the mast upright is to position your body away from the mast.

Recovering the rig

As the rig flips round, stabilise yourself to collect the rig. As the mast turns upright, do not lean outboard or expect the rig to support you — it won't. Do not lean outboard and reach for the boom. Keep low, force the mast forward, and only sheet in and commit the body to the rig when the boom is horizontal.

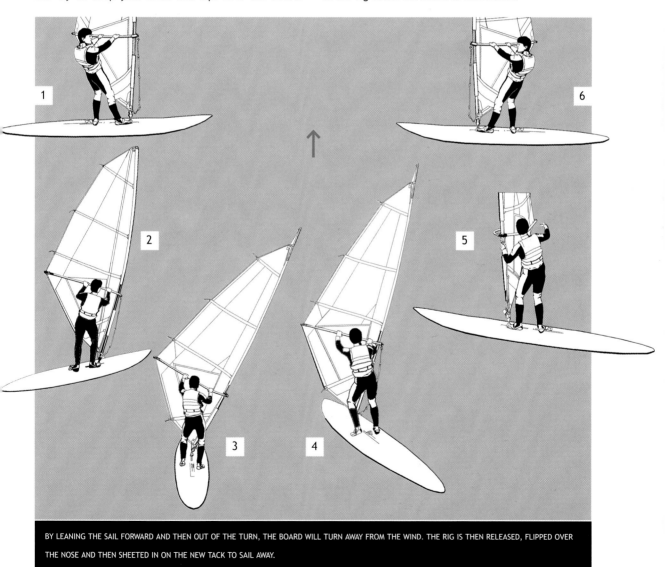

BY LEANING THE SAIL FORWARD AND THEN OUT OF THE TURN, THE BOARD WILL TURN AWAY FROM THE WIND. THE RIG IS THEN RELEASED, FLIPPED OVER THE NOSE AND THEN SHEETED IN ON THE NEW TACK TO SAIL AWAY.

Moving On

Once you have mastered the basics of technique that will keep you on the board, you can move onto more thrilling aspects such as speed, control, steering and sailing with a harness.

Controlling speed

When a board accelerates through its speed spectrum, the rig and sailor experience a metamorphosis — most noticeably when the board advances from nonplaning (displacing water like a boat) to planing (skimming over the top like a water ski) — with the increase in speed proportional to wind velocity. Many people hit a barrier at 10–12 knots (Force 4), when the board moves from a gentle glide to a faster pace known as 'planing' and needs little encouragement to accelerate with every gust. The body position that satisfied the rather tame demands of an upright rig when cruising won't work if you want to enjoy stronger winds and planing speeds. A change of attitude, foot placement and body position is required to control the forces as you accelerate.

To cope with stronger winds, identify your primary objectives: controlling the rig, committing properly to the harness, and resisting against a powerful sail. A direct result of implementing these 'improvements', makes the board travel faster. Once a board starts to plane, there is a shift of dynamics. As the wind picks up, the rig pulls harder and the board rides higher out of the water. To control the acceleration, your body has to react by moving back on the board. If you try to move back in light winds, the tail sinks. Yet, at speed, even a thin tail supports the heaviest of sailors.

PLANING THE COMBINATION OF POWERING THE SAIL UP AND SHEETING IN CONVERTS THE WIND'S STRENGTH INTO RAPID ACCELERATION. THIS, IN TURN, ENABLES YOU TO MOVE FURTHER BACK ON THE BOARD AND SETTLE INTO A MORE STABLE STANCE. BOTH FEET CAN MOVE BACK 30–45CM (12–18 INCHES) TOWARDS THE TAIL AND SLIGHTLY FURTHER OUT TO THE WINDWARD RAIL. THIS SHIFT COUNTERS THE SAIL'S PULL AND ENABLES THE BOARD TO PLANE MORE FREELY. A CLEAR SIGN OF THIS IS HOW THE FRONT OF THE BOARD IS RIGHT OUT OF THE WATER AND THE BOW WAVE IS NOW BACK IN LINE WITH THE MAST BASE.

NONPLANING WHEN YOU ARE TRAVELLING SLOWLY, THE RIG IS SHEETED OUT SLIGHTLY AND THE BODY IS WELL FORWARD. ALL YOUR BODY WEIGHT IS HEADING STRAIGHT DOWN THROUGH THE FEET ONTO THE BOARD. IF YOU STAY IN THIS POSITION AND THE WIND COMES UP, IT WOULD BE DIFFICULT TO RESIST THE RIG'S POWER, LEADING TO TREMENDOUS PULL ON THE ARMS AND A TENDENCY TO BE PULLED FORWARD.

Moving back for control

There are three main reasons to move back on the board as it accelerates.

■ A more rearward position reduces the chances of the board nose diving, which often leads to catapults.

■ Moving back counterbalances the extra power in the sail as the board picks up speed.

■ The action of moving back makes it easier to sheet the rig in and rake it back, enabling you to hold the power and remain on the plane.

Moving the feet and angling your body back uses your weight more effectively, making the action less physical and allowing you to enjoy the thrill of planing at speed. If you are looking to sail shorter boards, these all have straps at the back, so there is no avoiding the issue if you want to progress further.

Head and shoulders

Just as important as moving the feet back is leaning the head and shoulders out and back. This sheets the sail in through your body weight and pushes the board forward through your feet. If your head is directly over the feet, you have less leverage and gravity will pull the board down, preventing it from accelerating quickly.

When and how should I move back?

The basic rule is to move back as the board accelerates. The greater the speed, the further back you can move. A sudden move usually turns the board into wind, so make it a gradual, confident move.

To initiate the move, drop your hips towards the windward edge of the tail. If you simply walked back while still upright, the rig would sheet out and the lack of acceleration would mean the tail would not be able to support you. To steady yourself, take a small step towards the tail with your back foot, angling it slightly forward on the deck. Then wait and settle. Next, angle the whole body well past the back foot, as if you are pushing back into a sofa with your feet in front of you. You should feel the weight come off the front foot. Now lightly drag the front foot back, roughly to where your back foot is positioned. If you take the foot off the deck for too long, all your weight moves onto the back foot — which causes the board to luff — so slide it back gradually. Once the front foot is secure, widen your stance by stepping towards the tail with the back foot, so that your feet are separated comfortably. As a guide, your front foot ends up roughly where the back foot was (when standing upright in a nonplaning situation).

WITH YOUR FEET TO THE BACK OF THE BOARD AND YOUR HEAD AND SHOULDERS LEANING OUTWARD, YOU WILL FIND THAT THE SAIL SHEETS IN EASILY AND YOU HAVE MORE CONTROL OVER THE BOARD.

Why do I keep luffing into wind?

Firstly, don't move back unless the board feels like it is going to plane. If your sail is much smaller than that of most other sailors of your weight, the chances are that it will not support you and drive the board. But the most common way to reduce luffing is to keep the rig sheeted right in and your body back. This way, the front foot can push the board away from the wind with some force. Windsurfers who aren't afraid to go faster find it easier to prevent luffing. At speed, only gentle pressure through the front foot keeps it in check. The slower you move, the likelier you are to luff. If the board shoots off downwind as you move back, you are probably not far back enough and your feet are too far inboard, with insufficient weight on your heels.

The beach start

The beach start was developed to eliminate the difficulties of uphauling in the shorebreak. Wait until the tide has dropped or find the flattest area in which to practice. Even the smallest waves can break equipment, so avoid the impact zone by standing knee- or thigh-deep in the water, where the fin won't hit the bottom as you step on the board. If you go any deeper, you will need more wind to get you up and away. Remember, too, to start on the beach with the dagger board retracted, and follow the steps on pages 58–59.

Dry Land Practice

To improve your beach starts, try this simple experiment: From a sitting position in a chair, stretch both your feet right out in front of you. Now try to stand up! Difficult? Now bring the feet right close into the chair and stand up by rocking your head forward over your feet. Simple, but it's amazing how in the excitement of the whole process of starting on the beach, this simple point is neglected.

IDEAL CONDITIONS FOR A BEACH START ARE A GENTLY SHELVING BEACH WITH A CROSS-SHORE WIND.

TO AVOID LUFFING, YOU NEED TO ENSURE THAT THE RIG IS SHEETED IN AND THAT YOUR BODY IS POSITIONED BACK ON THE BOARD.

TURNING UPWIND TO TURN THE BOARD UPWIND, PULL THE FRONT HAND TOWARDS YOU WHILE DROPPING AND PUSHING THE BACK HAND AWAY TOWARDS THE TAIL OF THE BOARD. THIS DROPS THE RIG TOWARDS THE BACK OF THE BOARD AND PULLS ON THE MAST FOOT, BRINGING THE BOARD INTO WIND.

TURNING DOWNWIND TO TURN THE BOARD DOWNWIND, PUSH TOWARDS THE MAST BASE BY EXTENDING THE FRONT ARM. THIS WEIGHTS THE MAST BASE AND TURNS THE NOSE AWAY FROM THE WIND. FOR MORE SPEED, PULL IN AND LIFT WITH THE BACK HAND. THIS INCREASES THE WIND IN THE SAIL AND HELPS PUSH THE BOARD AWAY FROM THE WIND.

STEP 1 APPROACH THE WATER WITH THE BOARD AT RIGHT ANGLES TO THE WATER'S EDGE AND THE RIG DOWNWIND. TO KEEP THE SAIL CLEAR OF THE WATER, HOLD THE RIG BY THE BOOM AND LIFT IT TO HIP LEVEL. WALK INTO THE WATER, KEEPING THE RIG AS HIGH AS POSSIBLE.

STEP 2 STAND WINDWARD OF THE BOARD AND REST THE BOOM ON THE BACK OF THE BOARD. IDENTIFY WIND DIRECTION AND LEAVE THE BEACH AT RIGHT ANGLES TO IT. POINT THE NOSE INTO THE WAVES. IF THERE IS A SHOREBREAK DON'T BE CAUGHT BETWEEN THE BOARD AND BEACH.

3

STEP 3 RAISE THE RIG AND POSITION THE BOARD. YOU WILL SOON LEARN TO RECOGNIZE FROM THE PULL OF THE SAIL WHETHER THE ALIGNMENT OF BOARD, RIG AND SAILOR ARE CORRECT. IDEALLY, YOU SHOULD BE SLIGHTLY BEHIND THE BOARD RATHER THAN FACING IT.

4

STEP 4 TO START, HOLD YOUR BODY CLOSE TO THE TAIL, BUT REMEMBER THAT STEPPING STRAIGHT ONTO THE TAIL ONLY WEIGHTS ONE END OF THE SEE-SAW. WITH NO FORWARD MOMENTUM, AND NO WAY TO GENERATE ENOUGH MAST FOOT PRESSURE TO LEVEL THE BOARD, THE TAIL SINKS AND THE BOARD SPINS INTO THE WIND.

5

STEP 5 FOCUS EVERYTHING FORWARD AND TRY TO KEEP THE BOARD FLAT. PLACE THE BACK FOOT JUST BEHIND THE DAGGER BOARD, AND DO NOT PUSH THE SAIL UP TO ELEVATE THE RIG AS THIS WILL BACKWIND THE SAIL AND KILL THE LIFT.

6

STEP 6 MAKE SURE THAT THE NOSE IS OVER YOUR TOES BY LIFTING THE RIG UP AND FORWARD, STRAIGHTENING AND EXTENDING THE FRONT ARM AND SHEETING IN WITH THE BACK HAND. THIS CREATES A TWISTING MOTION THAT FORCES THE RIG UPRIGHT. THIS TWISTING FORWARD MUST COINCIDE WITH THE BODY'S FORWARD MOVEMENT INBOARD, WHICH IS INITIATED BY STEPPING UP ONTO THE BOARD OFF THE GROUNDED LEG. KEEP THE MAST FORWARD AND DOWNWIND OF THE NOSE.

FOCUS ON KEEPING THE BODY WEIGHT INBOARD, LOW AND TOWARDS THE MAST BASE, AND EXTEND THE ARMS UP. STEP RIGHT INBOARD AND HANG BELOW THE BOOM RATHER THAN PULL AGAINST IT FROM A VERTICAL POSITION. COMING UP ONTO THE BOARD, PLACE THE FRONT FOOT RIGHT UP NEAR THE MAST BASE, ANGLED FORWARD AND PUSHING THE BOARD FLAT.

The beach finish

Give yourself the time and space — 10–15m (33–50ft) — to prepare for a landing, and slow down! As you slow down, your fins may touch the ground, so be sure to finish in deep enough water (about waist deep).

Approaching the beach

The faster you are moving, the more upwind your approach should be. If the wind is dead onshore, head upwind and land almost pointing back out to the water. In cross-on, side-shore and slightly off-shore winds, head into wind. Always approach the shore on a close reach until the board has slowed down.

STEP 1 STEP OFF BEFORE THE FIN TOUCHES.

STEP 2 HOLD THE RIG ABOVE YOUR HEAD, WITH THE FRONT HAND ON THE MAST AND THE BACK HAND ON THE BOARD.

STEP 3 HEAD TOWARDS THE BEACH.

STEP 4 AS THE NOSE TOUCHES THE SHORE, TURN THE BOARD TOWARDS THE WIND UNTIL THE SAIL FLIPS OVER.

Stepping off

When heading into shallow water, sheet out with the back hand and drop your front foot alongside the windward rail so it is roughly in line with your back foot. If you are travelling fast, drop slowly and drag the foot.

Stepping down

Keep the rig slightly sheeted out and hang off the boom so most of your weight is directed into the mast base. Hold your body close to the board and bring the rig back towards the tail and over to windward. Prepare to step off with the back foot. Keep the rig slightly sheeted in with the back hand to support your weight and stop the mast toppling. Don't delay stepping off with the back foot or the board will run away. Stepping off towards the tail should leave the rig raked back over your head. Keep the rig low, with both hands on the boom to stop the wind catching it. Wait a second in preparation for the next move, adopt a slightly wider grip on the boom and try to keep a firm hold on the rig to prevent it from falling.

And back to land

To step back onto dry land, grasp the mast well above the boom with your front hand and, with your back hand, grab the tail or the back foot-strap. Lifting the tail, walk towards the beach. When you are almost out of the water, turn the tail and rig towards the wind, using the nose as the center of your turning circle. Keep turning around to windward, with the mast high and in front of the body. The rig should flip around. This is quite easy if you have a firm grip on the mast. With the board and rig having spun round 180°, you are able to drop the board and rig down in a start position.

Harnessing

Harnessing not only allows you to sail without tiring your arms too much, but also takes you into the world of planing and shorter boards. Every windsurfer has to master the harness once you have mastered sailing in winds up to a Force 3 (16kph/10mph). The harness not only gives you more time on the water, it also helps you sheet the boom in and rake the rig back.

Line positioning

Every time you use the harness, the lines need fine-tuning to suit the sail size and wind strength – especially if you use the same boom for different sails. If the wind increases (lines further back on the boom) or decreases (lines further forward), you will need to move the lines to accommodate the feel of the rig.

Analysing mistakes

Clues that indicate a fault with your lines:

Too far forward	Too far back
■ A strong pull on the back hand makes it difficult to let go without the sensation of hips being pulled inboard and forward or catapulted.	■ The board keeps heading up into wind.
■ The rig is hard to hold down and you are being pulled forward probably means that there is insufficient weight in the harness.	■ It feels like your body is being pulled inboard towards the tail.
■ A very strong pull on back hand in gusts or at speed.	■ There is a very strong pull on the front hand, despite moving both hands on the boom.
■ The sail won't sheet in when you sit down in the harness.	
■ You are having difficulty staying upwind.	

Positioning harness lines

THE LINE FIXING OF THE FRONT HARNESS SHOULD BE FASTENED ON THE BOOM NO FURTHER FORWARD THAN ELBOW (ON MAST) TO FINGERS, ALONG THE BOOM.

THE BIGGER THE SAIL OR THE MORE 'POWERED-UP' YOU ARE, THE FURTHER BACK THE HARNESS LINES SHOULD BE. THE REAR FIXING IS THEN POSITIONED A HAND-SPAN APART DOWN THE BOOM.

LINE LENGTH SHOULD BE ELBOW TO PALM FOR BEGINNERS USING LONG BOARDS IN MARGINAL WINDS. AS YOU GAIN EXPERIENCE – AND USE SHORTER BOARDS – YOU MAY REDUCE THE LENGTH OF THE LINE FROM ELBOW TO WATCHSTRAP. (THE BONY PART OF THE ELBOW LIES IN THE APEX OF THE LINE AND THE FIRST PART OF YOUR PALM RESTS ON THE OUTSIDE EDGE OF THE BOOM.)

Hooking in

Positioning the harness lines

It is impossible to position the lines correctly until you are on the water, because the wind on shore is never the same as on the water. Different makes of sail and variations in rigging mean that slight adjustments are always a part of harnessing.

If you can hook in and feel balanced when standing up near the mast base before sinking back in the harness and raking the rig back, then the lines are too far forward. Try sailing as fast as possible, with the rig raked back and sheeted in, but do not use the harness. Place your hands shoulder-width apart along the boom so that you can sheet the sail in. This will help you find the approximate center of effort.

See where the apex of the harness line is hanging in relation to your hook when you have the sail sheeted in and raked back. The apex should fall in front of the hook. If the line is further forward of your hook, or you need to twist your hips around towards the mast to hook in, the lines are too far forward.

Hooking in

Choose conditions that offer a steady breeze, with enough sail power to travel comfortably at speed. Too much wind will catapult you, while too little wind or a small sail will mean that there is nothing to support you. The aim is for your harness to carry all your weight and your arms are there to steer, not to hang from.

STEP 1 IN PRACTISING TO HOOK IN, HANG OUTBOARD AS FAR AS POSSIBLE. THIS FORCES THE RIG TO RAKE BACK AND BE SHEETED IN, AND BRINGS THE LINE TO WINDWARD OF THE BOARD AND TOWARDS YOU. IF YOU CAN HOLD THIS POSITION, YOU ARE READY TO HARNESS.

STEP 2 BY LIFTING THE HIPS AND USING A LIGHT PUMPING ACTION ON THE BOOM, THE LINE WILL FLICK TOWARDS YOU. AFTER A FEW ATTEMPTS, YOU WILL BE HOOKED IN. THEN SIT DOWN! DROP YOUR WEIGHT AND HIPS OUTBOARD. ENSURE THAT THERE IS CONSTANT TENSION IN THE LINE, OR IT WILL POP OUT.

STEP 3 DISTANCE YOURSELF FROM THE BOOM, SIT RIGHT BACK AND RELAX THE TENSION IN YOUR ARMS. AVOID BENDING THE ARMS OR THE LINE MAY DROP OUT. EQUALLY, IF A GUST HITS AND YOU DON'T SIT, THE RIG WILL PULL YOU UP ONTO YOUR TOES OR OVER ONTO THE RIG.

Sailing with a harness

Once you are hooked in, use your arms to sheet the rig in and out to control the power. Equally, if the board luffs, put the rig forward (slightly), and if the board shoots off downwind (common for those new to harnessing), lean the rig back to change direction.

To prevent a rather upright sailing stance, sink well into the harness. To help resist the power in the rig and adopt a more reclined position, drop your hips down and out, rather than just leaning back.

Using the harness requires more use of the feet to steer the board. If the board starts to luff, stay hooked in, drop your weight and push through the toes of the front foot to turn the board off the wind. If the board accelerates downwind, weight your heels and push through the back foot to bring the board upwind.

Unhooking the harness

It is easiest to unhook while still leaning outboard. If you come inboard to unhook, you will be lifted and it will be more difficult for the line to drop out. A sharp pull on the boom while still outboard is usually enough for the line to drop out.

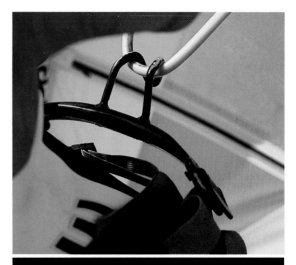

THE HARNESS SHOULD BE SAFELY SECURED TO YOUR RIG.

HARNESSING IS THE KEY TO STAYING ON THE WATER FOR LONG PERIODS, BUT YOU CAN ONLY POSITION THE LINES WHEN YOU ARE IN THE WATER.

Better harnessing

Once you have mastered hooking in and out and are sailing comfortably in the harness, you need to perfect your stance and make the harness work for you.

Stability and control are more attainable if the rig is positioned properly, so you need to lean into a committed body position to use the harness to your advantage.

When you connect to the line, the rig doesn't sheet in as easily with the lines forward, so the lines need to be short enough — and fixed far enough back on the boom — to ensure that the clew end of the boom is pulled in towards the tail of the board. If your body weight is hanging too far off the front of the boom, it will be more difficult to move back on the board.

Controlling the rig

Windsurfing rigs are designed to be sheeted in — ideally, so that the boom is almost parallel with the side of the board and the clew is raked back below the horizontal. If the rig is 'opened up', the board loses balance, drive and speed, and the rig loses stability.

Think of harness lines as a leverage tool. As the sail powers up, the back hand 'pull' increases. Compensate by shifting the harness lines further aft to relieve arm pressure, and sink back to keep the sail sheeted in. If you are sailing with the back hand well past the harness line, the lines are not far back enough.

Sheeting the rig in and raking it back

When new to harnessing, you may feel that your body is perfectly positioned with your backside skimming the water. But you may be wrong! In fact, your body may still be upright, the sail sheeted out, and too little weight through the harness. Unless you push yourself, it takes some time to realize how far you can, and should, commit in the harness. Your goal here is to drop your body weight in the harness.

Faults and problems

If the board luffs into wind while trying to move back or sit down in the harness, you are too heavily weighted on the back foot. To recover, sink lower and push through the front foot to turn the board off the wind. Sheeting the sail back in, by extending the front arm and pulling in with the back hand, should power the rig.

TO ACCELERATE, DISTANCE YOURSELF FROM THE BOOM WITH EXTENDED ARMS AND MOVE THE FEET OUT TO THE EDGE TO CONTROL SPEED. PUSHING OFF THE SIDE OF THE BOARD GIVES YOU MORE LEVERAGE AND RESISTANCE AND, AT THE SAME TIME, YOUR REAR SHOULDER AND ARM NEED TO BE DIRECTED OR 'DROPPED' OUT AND BACK, SO THAT YOUR SHOULDERS AND HIPS ARE PARALLEL WITH THE SIDE OF THE BOARD. THIS IS ALL DONE AS YOU SINK HARD AND LOW INTO THE HARNESS.

Final adjustments

You should be able to sail with both hands on each side of the harness fixings. Most beginners hold the boom with a wide grip — as if they are lifting weights. This reduces your sensitivity over the rig and prevents you finding the lines' balance. If your hands are on either side of the fixings and the back arm still pulls, or the sail is hard to sheet in, the lines are too far forward.

If the front hand pulls, try sheeting the sail in even more and if it still pulls, move the lines slightly forward. Don't be afraid to move the hands on the boom. A slight shift of the palms can relieve discomfort in the arms.

Harnessing is a constant trimming game. Minor line repositioning and a shift of the rig in the harness can rectify the situation. Finding the right position is not always immediate, but understanding the role of the harness is a good start. This dramatically increases your time on the water.

Footstraps

For the experienced sailor, footstraps are the interface with the board, allowing radical maneuvers while staying connected. For intermediates, they help maintain control and security on the board in planing conditions. To use footstraps, you need to be able to sail in a Force 4 and use a harness. If you cannot stand towards the back of the board at speed — and hooked in — you will *not* be able to use the straps properly. Fix the straps in the forward settings and use a single back strap on the back until you are proficient.

Getting into the straps

The first step is to make sure you are planing at speed and in the harness. Try to get as far outboard as possible, before going for the front strap. If you are standing inboard and above the strap it is hard to get your foot in without looking down — which often leads to the sail being sheeted out and immediately slows the board. When you are outboard, you have to stay sheeted in and it is easier to see the strap. If you find getting into the front strap difficult, you may have moved more upright and thus sheeted out.

STEP 1 BEFORE YOU EVEN ATTEMPT TO GET ON THE WATER, MAKE SURE THAT THE FOOTSTRAP IS TIGHT ENOUGH – BUT NOT TOO TIGHT – TO HOLD THE FOOT ON THE DECK OF THE BOARD. THE LITTLE TOE POKING THROUGH INDICATES A COMFORTABLE STRAP POSITION.

STEP 2 TO GET YOUR FRONT FOOT INTO THE STRAP YOU NEED TO 'UN-WEIGHT' AND LIFT YOUR FRONT FOOT OFF THE DECK. HAVING YOUR BACK FOOT BETWEEN THE FRONT AND BACK STRAPS SHOULD HELP YOUR BALANCE. WHEN REACHING FOR THE STRAP, REMAIN OUTBOARD AND SIT DOWN HARD IN THE HARNESS.

STEP 3 AS SOON AS THE FOOT IS IN THE STRAP, PUSH THE FRONT LEG FORWARD TO DRIVE THE BOARD ALONG. PROVIDED YOU STAYED SHEETED IN (IN OR OUT OF THE HARNESS), THE BOARD WILL REMAIN ON COURSE. IF YOU STAND UP AND SHEET OUT OR LEAN BACK AND DON'T PUSH THROUGH THE FRONT LEG, THE BOARD MAY LUFF.

STEP 4 WHEN YOU ARE IN THE FRONT STRAP, SIMPLY SAIL ON AND MAINTAIN SPEED. AIM TO SAIL WITH THE BACK FOOT CLOSE TO THE BACK STRAP; HOWEVER, IF YOU TRY TO PLACE THE BACK FOOT IN THE STRAP TOO SOON, YOU WILL SLOW DOWN. WAIT UNTIL YOU ARE PLANING PROPERLY IN THE HARNESS. IF THE BOARD GOES TOO FAST, HEAD UPWIND BEFORE REACHING FOR THE BACK STRAP.

STEP 5 PRIOR TO REACHING FOR THE BACK STRAP, 'UN-WEIGHT' THE BACK FOOT AND REMAIN OUTBOARD AND IN THE HARNESS TO KEEP THE SAIL SHEETED IN. HAVE YOUR BACK FOOT NEXT TO THE STRAP (NEVER STAND ON IT). BEND THE FRONT KNEE AND SLIDE YOUR FOOT INTO THE STRAP.

STEP 6 ONCE YOUR FOOT IS IN THE STRAP, RE-ESTABLISH AN OUTBOARD POSITION BY EXTENDING THE LEGS AND SINKING INTO THE HARNESS. ONCE YOU ARE IN BOTH STRAPS, YOU WILL HAVE MORE CONTROL IN STRONGER WINDS AND BE ABLE TO SAIL SHORTER BOARDS AT SPEED.

Sailing a Short Board

Short boards are used in stronger winds because their reduced length and lower volumes make them far more controllable. They are not only easier to turn, faster, and more exciting to ride, but enable windsurfers to enjoy a much wider range of wind and sea conditions.

Short board styles

Although there may be many different marketing terms to describe different styles of short boards, there are three main styles:

■ Slalom boards are for used blasting up and down on relatively flat water.

■ Free-ride boards are used largely for elaborate tricks.

■ Wave boards are largely for wave sailing and jumping in strong winds.

Most recreational sailors use slalom boards because they are easy to use and have various applications.

SHORT BOARDS VARY IN SIZE, VOLUME AND STYLES, FROM SLALOM AND WAVE BOARDS TO FREESTYLE.

Short board characteristics

Riding short boards usually demands more technical skill than the long board beginners tend to learn on. They have no dagger board — which makes them harder to keep upwind — and require planing winds (Forces 3–4 and above) to be sailed properly.

It is possible to sail short boards with larger volume (120l and more) and uphaul them, but you will still need to master the water start. Moving down onto shorter boards was once considered a major step but now, with the huge variety of high-volume short boards available, the progression can be more gentle.

On the water

Compared to long boards, short boards may appear to be more difficult to ride, and tend to be livelier and harder to keep upwind. The advantages, however, include their speed, maneuverability and, due to their smaller size, the possibility of venturing into the more extreme side of the sport: high-speed turns, jumping and wave riding. While you may never become an expert short-board sailor, these boards nevertheless offer great fun for the recreational sailor.

■ Board volume Always select a board that has enough volume to be uphauled (about 130l for most people over 70kg/155lb). As you improve, it is possible to sail smaller boards.

■ Footstraps and mast base Those new to footstraps should position them in the forward-most setting. The mast base should be placed in the track about 135–140cm (53–55 inches) from the tail.

■ Sail size Check to see that you are using a similar-sized sail to sailors who are of a similar size and build to you. Short boards need power.

opposite THE REDUCED SIZE AND VOLUME OF SHORT BOARDS MAKE THEM EASIER TO CONTROL IN WINDY CONDITIONS.

IT IS NOW POSSIBLE TO LEARN ON 'BEGINNER SHORT BOARDS'. THEY HAVE EXTRA VOLUME, AND THIS — ALONG WITH THE ADDITIONAL WIDTH — INCREASES STABILITY, ESPECIALLY IN WINDY CONDITIONS.

On the water

In any swell or strong wind, short boards are wobbly and difficult to uphaul, hence the need to 'water start' (see page 69). There is far less room for poor stance, board and rig trim, and the reduced volume and shorter waterline reduces stability, causing the board to stop and submerge at low speeds.

Although there are many different ways to sail a short board, most of the techniques already outlined in this volume may be appropriate to short-board sailing too.

The only real difference between short boards and long boards is their comparative instability (compared to more stable long boards), and all this means is that you will need to be more proficient at the basic skills before you venture onto boards with a volume of less than 130l. Nevertheless, there are at least two crucial moves that are an integral part of mastering the art of sailing a short board.

SHORT BOARDS WITH VOLUME LESS THAN 120 LITRES ARE MORE DYNAMIC AND REQUIRE A HIGHER LEVEL OF SKILL, OFFERING MORE SPEED AND FAR GREATER MANEUVERABILITY IN THE WATER.

The water start

Once you are sailing in winds of Force 4 and above, you will see just how beneficial water starting can be!

The water start essentially eliminates the hassle of uphauling, and vastly increases both safety and enjoyment on the water, particularly in conditions where there are strong winds. It is also a practical and useful skill for sailing in stronger winds on virtually any length of board, and an absolute 'must' for mastering (and maximum enjoyment) of short boards. As your water-starting proficiency grows, so will your confidence to tackle both shorter boards and conditions by which you were once daunted.

A water start is, in effect, a deeper-water beach start (see page 57) where the wind lifts you up onto the board, rather than you stepping up onto it. For your own safety, start learning the water start while still in your depth. This will allow you to learn the basics of the move while you are still able to easily reposition the board and/or rig when required. Shoulder-depth water is perfect. Don't be tempted to use too small a sail, since you will need power to pick you up and out of the water! A close-fitting buoyancy aid may also help, especially if you are not a strong swimmer. Only when you reach a 100-per-cent success rate should you move onto a board that cannot be uphauled.

STEP 1 THE BOARD IS AT RIGHT ANGLES TO THE WIND, AND THE MAST IS PULLED TOWARDS THE TAIL. THE SAIL IS RELEASED AND FILLS WITH WIND.

STEP 2 THE FRONT ARM PULLS THE RIG OVER THE HEAD AND WINDWARD.

STEP 3 THE WIND IN THE SAIL ALLOWS YOU TO BE SUPPORTED BY THE RIG.

STEP 4 AS SOON AS THE RIG IS RAISED, TREAD WATER, HOLDING THE SAIL ABOVE YOUR HEAD. IF YOU WANT TO TURN THE NOSE AWAY FROM THE WIND, PUSH WITH YOUR FRONT HAND AND PULL WITH THE BACK (AND VICE VERSA TO TURN INTO THE WIND).

STEP 5 WHEN THE BOARD IS RIGHT ANGLES TO THE WIND, YOU ARE READY. THE BACK FOOT MOVES ONTO THE BOARD AND THE RIG IS RAISED HIGHER.

STEP 6 BY RAISING THE RIG AND TWISTING IT FORWARD, THE SAIL IS EXPOSED TO THE WIND AND YOU WILL POP UP ONTO THE BOARD.

The carve jibe

One of the great attractions of sailing a short board is completing the high-speed turn commonly known as the 'carve jibe'. This move is a combination of 'carving' the board's inside rail into the water and releasing the rig over the nose of the board as it carves through the full 180° turn.

The action is similar to a standard jibe, but the board travels much faster and is banked to make it grip in the turn like a water ski. The move requires balance, timing and specific hand and foot movements, but with the right coaching and enough time on the water, carve gybing becomes a fast, fun way to turn the board around without stopping.

STEP 1 THE BOARD IS TURNED OFF THE DIRECTION OF THE WIND BY BEARING AWAY AT SPEED.

STEP 2 THE INSIDE RAIL IS PRESSED BY THE BACK FOOT AND THE BOARD STARTS TO CARVE.

STEP 3 WITH THE SAILOR AT FULL SPEED, THE BOARD REALLY BEGINS TO TURN ON THE WATER SURFACE.

STEP 4 AS THE BOARD CONTINUES THROUGH THE TURN, THE SAIL IS SHEETED OUT.

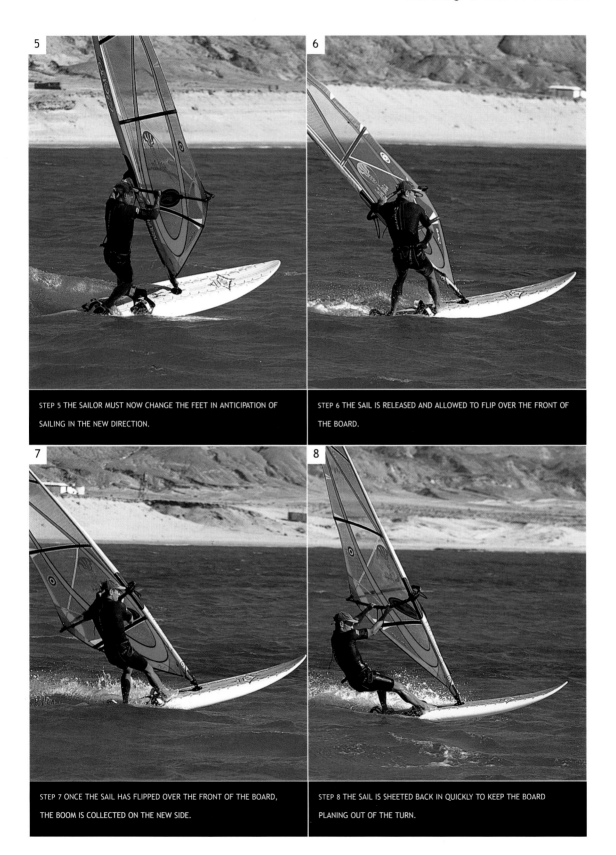

5

STEP 5 THE SAILOR MUST NOW CHANGE THE FEET IN ANTICIPATION OF SAILING IN THE NEW DIRECTION.

6

STEP 6 THE SAIL IS RELEASED AND ALLOWED TO FLIP OVER THE FRONT OF THE BOARD.

7

STEP 7 ONCE THE SAIL HAS FLIPPED OVER THE FRONT OF THE BOARD, THE BOOM IS COLLECTED ON THE NEW SIDE.

8

STEP 8 THE SAIL IS SHEETED BACK IN QUICKLY TO KEEP THE BOARD PLANING OUT OF THE TURN.

Advanced Windsurfing

for most windsurfers, sailing in a moderate breeze with a few friends is pleasure enough, but for those driven by the thrill of competition, advanced windsurfing is the only antidote.

Competitive windsurfing

Amateur racing is organized by the International Funboard Class Association in 43 countries and comprises a series of competitions held over a year. Entry is open to anyone who wants to gain a national ranking.

The cream of competitions is the PWA (Professional Windsurfing Association) World Tour, which travels the globe every year searching for the most ideal racing conditions. There are separate competitions for men and women, and a variety of disciplines, namely: slalom and course racing, wave sailing and freestyle. Each discipline earns the competitors points — and a

slice of the US$2 million prize money. A typical year will take in 10–15 different venues, selected for their suitability for one of the disciplines. These truly cover the globe, taking in Brazil, the Canary Islands and Europe, and the windsurfing calendar ends with a Big Wave contest at Hookipa Beach Park in Maui.

The competitors

Only the world's top 250 ranked sailors are eligible to enter the PWA tour but not all members enter every event or discipline; some specialize in either the racing or wave/freestyle contests. Generally, the larger, heavier sailors favor the power and speed of racing, while the lighter sailors tend to excel in the waves. Each discipline has its own champions but, to be world champion, you must excel in all four — rather like having to race a Formula One car and a rally car to be crowned World Motor-racing Champion. The world championship is an impressive achievement and has been claimed by only three people: Robby Naish, who was world champion for five consecutive years before being superseded by Bjorn Dunkerbeck, who took a firm grip on the title for a record-breaking 12 years. The most recent champion is Kevin Pritchard of the USA.

Indoor windsurfing

Indoor windsurfing is a special PWA event that only a few of the best, and most foolhardy, professionals enter. The venue is a giant pool, 90m/295ft in length, in which 16 sailors perform time trials to qualify for subsequent four-man heats around the pool's perimeters. One after another, the sailors launch themselves down a start ramp sloped at 40° into 30-knot winds artificially generated by giant electric fans. The sailors have only seconds to get their bearings before they are forced to jibe around the first buoy and then again and again. Each race lasts little more than a minute but demands both nerves of steel and incredible fitness from the sailors. The rigs and boards (customized for the event) often break and injuries are not uncommon, although padded mats alongside the pool cushion competitors who find themselves making unexpected exits.

above IMPRESSIVE MANEUVERS BY PARTICIPANTS IN PWA WORLD TOUR EVENTS USUALLY ATTRACT ENTHUSIASTIC SPECTATORS.

opposite A PROFESSIONAL SHOWS OFF A BREATH-TAKING STUNT.

The champions
Bjorn Dunkerbeck

Standing 1.6m (5ft 3 inches) tall and weighing a hefty 96kg (212lb), Bjorn Dunkerbeck's strength and power has put him streaks ahead in competitive racing, especially in extreme conditions. Together with the consistency of his skilled performance, his complete fitness and perfect board and rig control, Dunkerbeck has deservedly gained himself a reputation for being virtually unbeatable.

Robby Naish

Robby Naish won his first world championship when he was 13 years old and it was clear from those early days that he was a legend in the making. Naish joined the pioneers who took windsurfing into the Hawaiian waves and, as the professional element of the sport developed, Robby Naish flourished with dynamic moves and radical performances. He soon became the first 'star' of wind-

ROBBY NAISH

surfing and remains the favorite of many windsurfing enthusiasts to this day. Famed for his creativity and excellence in the waves, Robby Naish, his board and sail brands are now synonymous with the sport.

Karin Jaggi

Landlocked Switzerland may not be the obvious breeding ground for a world windsurfing champion, but in 1998 Karin Jaggi put her country on the map by winning the women's World Cup title. Renowned for her strength and fierce determination, Karin is one of the best-known female sailors in the world, with a string of speed-sailing, wave-sailing and racing titles to her name. Besides a reputation as the world's number one racer, she is also known for her love of wild maneuvers, including push loops, Vulcans, aerial jibes and one-handed table tops. Her main ambition is to be the first woman to pull off a double forward maneuver.

BJORN DUNCKERBECK

KARIN JAGGI

Racing

There are two types of race events: course racing, which is normally reserved for winds of 8–20 knots, and slalom, which usually takes place in winds of more than 20 knots.

Course racing

For the course racing event, a fleet of up to 64 wind-surfers compete at the same time over a marked course. Similar to yacht racing, the competitors race upwind and then downwind, often completing a number of tactical laps. The races last up to half an hour. To maximize the lighter winds, racers use high-volume short boards and rigs of up to 10m (33ft) in size.

SUCCESS IN DOWNWIND SLALOM REQUIRES NERVES OF STEEL. ONE ERROR IN TURNING AT THE MARK SPELLS DISASTER.

Slalom racing

Slalom racing is especially fast and furious. Run in quick-fire, 3- to 4-minute heats, eight sailors race downwind around a series of buoys (much like a large water ski slalom course). It is close, exciting racing at high speeds of 50kph (30mph), with plenty of crowded jibes close to the shore to entertain spectators. This is a knock-out contest, with the top four sailors in each heat moving into the next round. The organizers try to run the slalom in high winds and even through waves, so racers generally choose small boards and rigs to give them control for the tight turns and blistering winds.

A COURSE IS SET SO THAT THE RACERS ARE FORCED TO SAIL CLOSE TO EACH OTHER.

Wave sailing

Wave sailing combines a board's natural surfing properties with the power of a sail. This is windsurfing's most radical event and takes place in some of the world's biggest wave locations. Competitors have approximately 12 minutes to impress judges with their ability to 'ride' and 'jump', with points awarded for innovation, style and handling of the conditions.

When riding a wave, the aim is to sail for as long as possible along the face of the wave, close to the breaking point, before turning at the bottom and cutting back up in a series of hair-raising, winding maneuvers. On the way out, competitors jump off the top of the breaking waves, projecting high into the air (up to 12m/40ft). As if that were not enough in itself, the most radical wave sailors will perform contorted moves that involve 360° spins, loops and other gravity-defying maneuvers.

WITH WAVES THE SIZE OF HOUSES, 50KPH (30MPH) WINDS AND HIGH-ALTITUDE JUMPS, WAVE COMPETITIONS ARE NOT FOR THE FAINT-HEARTED. HAILED AS THE SPORT'S MOST DEMANDING STYLE, WAVE SAILING REQUIRES EXTRAORDINARY SKILL ON THE PART OF THE SAILOR.

Freestyle

Freestyle was introduced to the PWA circuit in 1998 and allows sailors to show off their rig and board-handling talents away from huge waves. 'Freestylers' perform fast, dynamic moves in unexploited locations, such as inland water. There are an endless combination of sail spins, pirouettes and skateboard-style moves that are judged on difficulty, fluidity and style.

top THE PERFORMANCE OF FREESTYLERS DEPENDS LITTLE ON THE QUALITY OF WAVES, SO FREESTYLE IS POPULAR ON INLAND WATERS.

above WITH GIANT WAVES AND HIGH WINDS, THE GRAVITY-DEFYING JUMPS SEEN IN WAVE COMPETITIONS REQUIRE EXPERT HANDLING SKILLS.

OLYMPIC COMPETITORS USE STANDARD BOARDS, SO TECHNIQUE AND TACTIC COUNT MORE THAN FASTER EQUIPMENT.

For the record

The search for new challenges and the impulse to break barriers has led windsurfers across the oceans, constantly trying to reach faster and faster speeds. At specialized speed events, where entrants take the biggest sail they can handle in gale-force winds, speeds of over 45 knots have been achieved.

Olympic windsurfing

Windsurfing has been an Olympic sport since 1984 but, unlike PWA competitions, this is a one-design class, where competitors use identical boards and sails. (The Olympic committee is considering making changes to the design specifications of the board to account for developments in the sport in recent years.) Selection for the national teams is highly contested, with only one sailor being selected every four years. Due to the fact that the Olympics involves only course racing, it is highly tactical and there are many Olympic special-ists who spend years training to reach the optimum weight for the board. To stand a chance of winning gold in Olympic windsurfing, sailors have to be super fit (the first Olympics didn't allow harnesses) and weigh about 70kg (154lb), which is why the heavier PWA sailors don't usually compete.

Transatlantic Windsurfing Race

Organized by the PWA, this unique event is the ulti-mate test of endurance and stamina, in which sailors race 4,000km (2,500) miles across the Atlantic. The first race, in 1999, took competitors from Canada to the UK. The repeat race from Portugal to Brazil in 2000 had to be abandoned after rescue boats found that they could not cope with the conditions. The wind-surfers, however, were fine!

WINDSURFERS HAVE RACED ACROSS HUGE TRACTS OF WATER, NONE MORE CHALLENGING THAN THE PIONEERING TRANSATLANTIC WINDSURFING RACE FIRST HELD IN 1999.

Enjoying
the Ride

Your experience and enjoyment of windsurfing will depend on a number of elements — all of which are well in within your control. Rule number one is always safety first, but you will also need to consider other important issues, such as weather conditions, your own skills and abilities, and the quality and state of your equipment.

above IT IS ALWAYS MORE ENJOYABLE AND SAFER TO SAIL WITH SOMEONE ELSE — ALTHOUGH IT IS NOT A GOOD IDEA TO SAIL AS CLOSE AS THIS. SAFETY SHOULD TAKE PRECEDENCE OVER THE THRILL.

opposite BEING ALONE ON THE WATER CAN BE FUN, BUT A LONE SAILOR NEEDS TO BE ESPECIALLY AWARE OF POTENTIAL HAZARDS.

Safety first

Many of the main self-rescue points you will need to know are covered on page 27, but you may need additional pointers on safety to make your time on and off the water safer and more enjoyable. Out on the water, you will inevitably encounter obstacles, which could lead to trouble, and possibly even collide with other watersport enthusiasts — especially as a beginner — so it is always a good idea to familiarize yourself with first aid. In addition, in order to enjoy the adventure of the sport, you may also need tips on diet and exercise, which help maintain your body and level of fitness so that you can fully appreciate the experience.

Maritime rules

While windsurfing is generally performed in areas of open water, you may nevertheless still come into close contact with other craft. Even though the rule that 'power gives way to sail' still holds true, it is best to avoid all powered pleasure or commercial craft. They are far less manoeuvrable than a windsurfer and much harder to stop. Drifting out into a shipping lane is a very serious issue, so avoid venturing into areas where this could become a problem.

You are more likely to be sailing close to other windsurfers and small sail-powered craft, but colliding at speed can be still be dangerous — and very expensive.

Insurance

Third-party insurance is a must for every windsurfer. If you are hiring equipment from a recognized windsurfing school, check that insurance is part of the package. If you purchase your own board, it is vital that you gain cover against accidents with other water users. A good windsurfing shop will be able to advise you on companies that specialize in this service.

THIS WINDSURFER IS SAILING ON PORT TACK.

THIS WINDSURFER IS SAILING ON STARBOARD TACK.

Port tack

If you are sailing on 'port tack' (with the wind blowing over the left-hand side of the board and the left hand facing forward on the boom), then you are required to give way. If two boards are travelling together on the same tack, the board to windward (closest to the wind) must keep clear when overtaking.

When venturing into waves, a sailor heading out through the oncoming waves has right of way over those riding the waves in.

Starboard tack

Starboard has right of way. When the wind is blowing over the right-hand side of the board (and your right hand is nearest the mast), you are on 'starboard tack' and have right of way over another vessel heading towards you. You should hold your course; the other vessel is obliged to move out of your way. Hopefully, the other water users also will know this simple rule. If they don't, raise your voice and call 'Starboard!' — rather official, but they should understand what you mean.

WHENEVER YOU ARE SAILING WITH OTHERS — BE IT COMPETITIVELY OR SIMPLY RECREATIONAL — IT IS ESSENTIAL THAT YOU ARE AWARE OF BASIC MARITIME RULES THAT APPLY TO WATER 'TRAFFIC'.

Good harness technique not only saves energy and adds comfort, but is also the safest way to sail. If the harness is kept tight, you can sail safe in the knowledge that your line length will remain constant. There is bound to be some slack when you sink hard into the harness, but minimal movement shows both a well-fitting and adjusted harness.

■ Loosely position your harness, using the waist strap to hold it in place. The design will determine hook height, but the spreader bar (see page 95) lies at about your belly button.

■ Without cutting off the blood supply to the legs, tighten both legstraps. This secures the harness position and stops it riding up as you tighten the spreader.

■ The last — and crucial — step is to tighten the spreader bar as much as you can. If you have a quick-release system, tighten it again after clipping in.

■ If the spreader bar touches both buckles and prevents tightening any further, invest in a smaller spreader bar.

■ All straps stretch when wet, so the harness will need retightening at every session.

A CHEST HARNESS SUPPORTS THE SHOULDERS AND LOWER BACK.

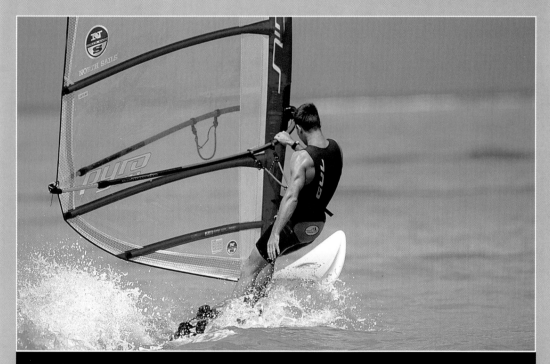

INITIALLY, SETTING THE HARNESS LINES MAY SEEM DIFFICULT, BUT IT BECOMES EASIER OVER TIME. SOON YOU WILL BE ABLE TO SAIL AND TAKE ONE HAND OFF AND RELAX IN THE HARNESS.

WEARING SUNBLOCK OR EVEN A HAT WILL PROTECT YOU FROM THE HARSH RAYS OF THE SUN WHILE OUT ON THE OPEN WATER.

First aid

There is little chance of injury in recreational windsurfing. Provided you sail within your limits, you may receive a few knocks and bruises during a fall. Professionals who attempt aerial moves take higher risks and suffer twisted ankles during falls or in breaking waves.

Emergencies

If you ever see anyone who looks as if they could be in distress, always ask if they need assistance and call for emergency services as soon as possible. It may, therefore, be a good idea to familiarize yourself with the International Distress Signal (see page 28).

Sunburn

One of the most common ailments for sailors is sunburn. Overexposure to the sun while out in the fresh breeze and cool water is not easy to detect, so always use a high-strength sunblock. There are plenty of water-resistant creams and lotions available, which will provide adequate protection from the sun. Wearing a hat is also an option, but you may need to tie it on!

Hypothermia

Hypothermia is considerably more serious than simple sunburn. Most vulnerable are those sailing in colder climates, but hypothermia is always a risk if you spend too much time in the water, and is particularly common among sailors rescued from difficult situations. It is an error to assume that you do not need a wetsuit because the sun is out. Especially in cooler climates, a wetsuit can save you life.

Food and drink

Because windsurfing is an active sport that requires considerable energy, your diet will inevitably affect your sailing. If you know you will be spending a lot of time on the water, eat plenty of energy-providing carbohydrates (such as pasta and rice) the night before. More importantly, drink plenty of liquid during breaks on the water. Being well hydrated will enable you to sail for much longer. When you are windsurfing in hot climates, this should amount to no less than 2–3l (3$^{1}/_{2}$–5 pints) of water a day. And don't forget to eat during your breaks!

Exercises for windsurfing

Even if you can only find time at the weekends or on holiday to enjoy the rigors of the sport, having a good level of fitness will play a large part in your enjoyment and progression through the learning curve. If you combine the exercises depicted here with regular, aerobic activity, such as cycling, walking, swimming or running, you'll be better prepared for your windsurfing sessions.

However, it is essential — as with all sudden or gradual changes to your standard exercise regime — that you check with a doctor before you attempt any exercises that have not specifically been recommended by your physician.

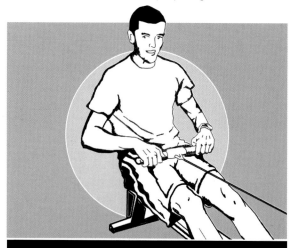

WINDSURFING PROFESSIONALS USE A ROWING MACHINE TO ACHIEVE A GOOD AEROBIC WORKOUT AND DEVELOP UPPER BODY MUSCLES.

above HANGING FROM A BAR AND DOING A SERIES OF PULL-UPS IS AN EXCELLENT WAY TO IMPROVE YOUR STAMINA ON THE WATER. IF YOU FIND IT DIFFICULT TO LIFT YOUR BODY WEIGHT, PLACE YOUR FEET ON A STOOL IN FRONT OF YOU TO REDUCE SOME OF THE STRAIN.

above right ROPE ROLLING STRENGTHENS THE FOREARMS, HANDS AND WRISTS. TIE A 30CM (1FT) PIECE OF OLD BOOM — OR BROOM HANDLE — TO A 1.5M (5FT) LENGTH OF ROPE. ATTACH THE OTHER END OF THE ROPE TO A 0.5–5KG (1–10LB) WEIGHT. WITH THE ARMS OUTSTRETCHED OR BENT AT APPROXIMATELY 90°, ROLL THE BAR IN THE PALM OF YOUR HAND TO SHORTEN THE ROPE AND LIFT THE WEIGHT FROM THE GROUND. BEFORE LONG, YOUR FOREARMS, HANDS AND WRISTS WILL BE HIGHLY DEVELOPED, AND EVEN YOUR PALMS WILL HAVE HAD A WORKOUT IN THE PROCESS.

Winds and weather
The wind is influenced by the world's weather patterns, so being able to read and understand changing weather patterns will help you find the right time and place to windsurf – and avoid problems.

Understanding wind patterns
Wind is generated by the difference in atmospheric pressure between areas of high and low pressure. Weather maps show these in the form of isobars. In areas of high pressure the isobars are far apart. Isobars that are close together indicate a low-pressure system. High-pressure systems move relatively slowly and usually mean more settled, calm weather and lighter winds. Low-pressure systems move much faster and absorb warm air from tropical regions and cool air from polar regions. These develop into what is known as 'fronts' as the isobars pack tightly together. If the weather chart looks rather like a dart board, you know you are in for very windy weather.

The wind generally travels in the same direction as the isobars. In the northern hemisphere the wind blows anticlockwise around a low-pressure system, and vice versa in the southern hemisphere.

SAILING IN POWERFUL WINDS IS WINDSURFING AT ITS MOST DANGEROUS AND IS ONLY FOR PRACTICED EXPERTS.

In locations that rely on less predictable weather fronts and low-pressure systems to deliver the stronger winds, it can mean plenty of waiting and searching for wind. Telephone 'wind-lines', and Web-cams linked to websites are now being introduced at popular sites to give those travelling in over long distances the opportunity to check wind conditions before leaving home.

Trade and thermal winds
The most reliable winds are the trades (see page 86) that make locations such as the Caribbean and Hawaii so popular among windsurfers. The other type of wind is the thermal wind or 'sea breeze'. These come about because of the difference in heat between the water and the surrounding area. As the land heats up, the air above it rises, causing a thermal effect as the cooler air comes in off the water to replace the rising hot air on the land. This process is particularly effective in very hot locations, such as mid-summer in the Mediterranean, where the wind is very light in the mornings and then strengthens during the day as the land heats up. This effect works even in cold-water areas such as lakes and rivers, provided there is some difference in temperature between the water and land.

Tides, currents and local conditions
The tide varies around the world. In northern European locations, the rise and fall can be many metres, while in the Caribbean, it may only be a few feet. The tides go up and down according to the gravitational pull of the moon. This causes the tide to flow in and out roughly every 12 hours. Tides can be incredibly strong and, when combined with a fresh wind, they cause standing waves and challenging conditions.

It is also possible to sail in venues where the tide will affect the extent of the sailing area. The rise and fall of the tide can be so great that, when the tide is right out, the seabed, rocks and reefs are exposed. Local tide tables explain the tide's daily time and range.

Be wary of outgoing tides and strong currents that might be caused by local headlands, river mouths, rocks or underwater obstacles – yet another reason to windsurf where there are others on the water.

BEAUFORT SCALE

Wind force	Wind speed (knots)	Wind description	Wave height	On the sea	On the land
0	0–1	Calm	0	Flat, mirror-like sea	Smoke creates vertical column
1	1–3	Light air movement	0.1m (⅓ft)	Scale-like ripples, but no crests of foam	Wind direction indicated by smoke, but weather vanes not affected
2	4–6	Light breeze	0.5m (1½ft)	Wavelets, with glass-like crests that do not break	Weather vanes move, leaves rustle
3	7–10	Gentle breeze	1m (3½ft)	Larger wavelets, with crests that begin to break; glassy foam, and occasional white horses	Noticeable movement of leaves and twigs
4	11–16	Moderate breeze	2m (6½ft)	Small waves, with regular white horses	Movement of branches and debris/litter, with some dust
5	17–21	Fresh breeze	3m (10ft)	Moderate waves, which are longer and with many white horses; some spray	Noticeable movement in small trees; inland water has small wavelets with crests
6	22–27	Strong breeze	4m (13ft)	Large waves, with extensive white foam crests; some spray	Noticeable movement of large branches; clear gusts of wind
7	28–33	Near gale	5m (16½ft)	Choppy sea, with white foam crests blown in streaks	Trees sway, and walking upwind is difficult
8	34–40	Gale	6m (19½ft)	Relatively high waves, with crest edges beginning to break into spindrift; foam forms noticeable streaks	Trees lose branches, and walking upwind is very difficult
9	41–47	Strong gale	7m (23ft)	High waves, with clear foam streaks; crests begin to tumble and fall; visibility affected by sea spray	Some damage to structures such as roofs and chimneys
10	48–55	Storm	9m (30ft)	Very high waves, with long, curved crests that result in large areas of white streaks of foam; heavy tumbling; visibility noticeably affected	Whole trees uprooted; considerable structural damage

Explore the World

Windsurfers go everywhere: from the sheltered bays of the Virgin Islands, to the fearsome reefs of Fiji and scenic lakes of Europe. In fact, wherever there is an accessible stretch of water, wind and daylight, you can be guaranteed to find windsurfers enjoying the freedom of their sport.

Windsurfing hotspots

Some locations have become renowned for their outstanding conditions and facilities, and attract thousands of visiting windsurfers looking for reliable wind. Some have become legendary for their fast waves and strong winds that test expert windsurfers to the limit, but many others offer a much wider range of conditions. In these places, you may find experienced windsurfers sailing in challenging waves, while a little further down the coast, beginners and intermediates are happily practising many of the more basic skills!

There are hundreds of fully catered centers and windsurfing resorts, offering a widest selection of hire equipment and tuition. Specialized windsurfing holiday companies can advise you on the right holiday center to match your level of expertise.

Following the wind

Some destinations boast strong, consistent wind all year round, while others have particular seasons.

■ World trade winds are the most reliable and bless many windsurfing locations, such as the Caribbean and Hawaii. Here, winds remain virtually constant all year.

■ Thermal winds build up during the day. The land heats up, causing the air to rise. Cooler air comes in off the water, replacing the hot air. This thermal wind may top up existing wind and create a strong effect. Lake Garda in Italy, and the USA's Columbia River Gorge and San Francisco Bay have very regular thermal winds.

■ A catabatic wind known as 'Eric' affects the mountain-enclosed bay of Vassiliki in Greece. 'Eric' falls down the mountain side and blows across the bay in the afternoon, before receding up the mountain in the evening. So well defined is the line of wind that a beginner may sail in light winds on the far side of the bay, while experienced sailors scream up and down a few hundred yards upwind.

RECOGNIZED WINDSURFING CENTERS WORLDWIDE OFFER TUITION, HIRING FACILITIES AND ADVICE — ESPECIALLY HELPFUL IF YOU ARE NEW TO THE SPORT OR UNFAMILIAR WITH THE LOCATION.

SOME WINDSURFING CENTERS ARE COMBINED WITH DINGHY SAILING CENTERS. MANY OF THESE ARE BASED IN THE MEDITERRANEAN AND THEIR FAVORABLE WINDS ARE POPULAR WITH BEGINNERS.

WINDSURFING CAN BE FUN ON EVEN THE COLDEST OF WINDSWEPT BEACHES. HERE SPECTATORS WATCH A WORLD CUP EVENT IN NORTHERN EUROPE. NO BOARD SHORTS HERE!

Northern Europe

Virtually every northern European country has a range of suitable windsurfing venues. In most cases, the stronger winds are from irregular weather systems, which generally means lower temperatures (especially from autumn to spring), and the need of a wetsuit to combat the cooler winds and water.

The Mediterranean

Mediterranean shores offer the widest ranges of windsurfing holidays and locations. There are literally hundreds of windsurfing schools and rental sites dotted along the entire coastline and on most of the islands. The more famous include Vassiliki in Greece (see page 86), which is perfect for beginners; Tarifa, a World Cup venue with strong winds and a speed course; and the Greek island of Karpathos, possibly one of the windiest locations in the world, so not a good place to learn basic skills. Other popular locations include Rhodes and Kos in Greece, Northern Sardinia, Paros and Crete.

WARM WINDS, SUNSHINE AND BLUE WATERS ARE A WINDSURFER'S DREAM, WHICH IS WHY LOCATIONS SUCH AS THE MEDITERRANEAN AND CARIBBEAN ARE SO POPULAR AS WINDSURFING HOLIDAY DESTINATIONS.

Egypt

Since the early 1990s, Egypt has rapidly developed as a popular windsurfing destination for many Europeans. The heat from the desert means that the wind is extremely consistent from April through to October, and still stays warm with regular winds from November through to March (unlike the Mediterranean). The most popular locations in Egypt include Dahab and Moon Beach on the Sinai Peninsula, and Hurghada and Safaga on the Red Sea.

The Canary Islands

The Canary Islands, a group of seven remote islands off the coast of North Africa, are a veritable windsurfing playground, in particular the islands of Gran Canaria, Fuertaventura, Lanzarote and Tenerife. All these islands have, at some time or another, hosted World Cup events and offer an exceptional variety of conditions.

Gran Canaria, home to past world champion Bjorn Dunkerbeck, is famed for a super-windy, hostile beach at Pozo, littered with large boulders and blasted by winds of up to 50 knots in the summer months. When the PWA tour is in town, the best sailors in the world risk all, attempting 9–12m (30–40ft) jumps and double loops only metres off the beach.

MANY CENTERS HAVE THEIR HIRE EQUIPMENT RIGHT ON THE BEACH, WITH ONLY A SHORT WALK TO THE WATER AND NO NEED FOR RIGGING.

Fuertaventura boasts excellent waves in the north, and many speed records have been broken at Sotavento beach. The neighboring islands of Tenerife (El Medano) and Lanzarote (Las Cucharas) offer varied conditions.

South Africa

South Africa, with miles of beautiful coastline, is steadily growing as a windsurfing destination between November and March. The favorite spots include Blouberg in Table Bay for waves, and Langebaan on the West Coast for flat water and easier conditions.

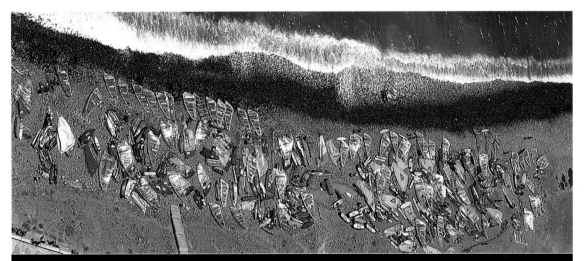

THE MORE POPULAR WINDSURFING BEACHES CAN BECOME RATHER CROWDED — ESPECIALLY WHEN A COMPETITION IS IN PROGRESS — AND THE SHORES ARE LITTERED WITH BOARDS, RIGS AND AND AN ENDLESS SEA OF SPECTATORS.

The Caribbean

Warm waters, steady trade winds and easy conditions have brought the Caribbean chain of islands to the forefront of windsurfing, from the windy islands of the north Venezuelan coast right up to the more tranquil Virgin Islands.

Margarita, Aruba, Bonaire, Barbados, Antigua, Tobago, Dominican Republic, the Virgin Islands and Puerto Rico all have windsurfing centers and equipment for all levels of expertise. The northern part of the Caribbean is more reliable for wind and weather from April to September, after which the trades shift south and favor the islands lower down in the extensive chain.

The United States of America

In a country as vast and expansive as the USA, windsurfers will find hotspots to suit every level of performance. The most popular and respected venues in the USA include Cape Hatteras on the east coast, which sports both waves and flat water, and San Francisco on the west coast, with its impressive backdrop of the Golden Gate Bridge and Alcatraz. However, the most famous and impressive venue of all is The Gorge. Situated on the Columbia River, this huge river is a unique windsurfing phenomenon. The current runs in the opposite direction to the very reliable winds (from April to September), enabling you to sail all day without ever worrying about drifting downwind.

MANY CARIBBEAN ISLANDS OFFER THE PERFECT WINDSURFING LOCATION, SOME OF WHICH HAVE HOSTED A NUMBER OF BOTH PROFESSIONAL AND AMATEUR EVENTS.

EACH YEAR, HUNDREDS OF SPECTATORS GATHER TO WATCH THE WORLD'S BEST WAVE SAILORS COMPETE AT THE WINDSURFING MECCA OF HOOKIPA IN HAWAII.

The paradise of Hawaii

If there is indeed a Mecca for windsurfing, it has to be Maui in the Hawaiian chain of islands in the Pacific. The trade winds are so reliable and the conditions so varied that most of the world's top windsurfers live and train here. Easy conditions may be found at Kanaha Beach Park on the north coast and Kehei on the south coast, particularly through the summer, from April to September. However, Maui earned its reputation from its huge waves. When the winter swells hit the islands, the shallow reefs throw up some of the most demanding conditions. Hookipa Beach Park is famous the world over, but only 8km (5 miles) up the coast is 'Jaws'. This monster wave can tower as high as three or four masts and is only accessible to the most fearless of sailors, who are prepared to risk their lives and equipment to ride the huge swell.

AUSTRALIA HAS EXCELLENT FLAT-WATER WINDSURFING, BUT WESTERN AUSTRALIA IS PARTICULARLY FAMOUS FOR ITS FANTASTIC WAVES, WHICH OFFER EXPERT SAILORS A THRILLING VIEW OF THE DRAMATIC COASTLINE.

NEW ZEALAND'S FINEST COMPETITIVE WINDSURFERS REPRESENTED THEIR COUNTRY IN THE 2000 OLYMPIC GAMES IN SYDNEY, AUSTRALIA.

Australia

Australia probably has as many windsurfing locations as the rest of the world put together, but the vastness of the country and limited population means that only a few areas have become well known.

Western Australia, in particular, offers a variety of conditions for all levels that rival many of the other famous spots worldwide, and include Geraldton, Lancelin and Margaret River. Generally considered more reliable for wind between November and April, Western Australia offers the more adventurous windsurfer perfect, uncrowded locations with warm winds and clear water.

New Zealand

New Zealand is one of the least populated windsurfing destinations, with Wellington one of the most popular spots for flat-water conditions, especially for beginners and intermediates. Experienced sailors head for Taranaki, a much-favored spot in the southwest of North Island blessed with regular winds.

Making contact

Professional and national windsurfing associations are usually staffed by experienced windsurfers who have considerable insight into conditions and facilities in their particular region, and can offer sound advice as well as contact information to help you plan your trip.

PROFESSIONAL WINDSURFING ASSOCIATIONS

UNITED KINGDOM
- SSM FREESPORTS
- The Green Room, 1 Buston Road, London SW15 6AR, England
- E-mail: info@ssm-freesports.com

UNITED STATES OF AMERICA
- WINDSURFING USA
- Website: www.windsurfingmag.com
- E-mail: windsurf@worldzine.com

AUSTRALIA
- AUSTRALIAN WINDSURFING ASSOCIATION
- Website: www.windsurfing.org
- E-mail: phil.jones@bigpond.com

NATIONAL WINDSURFING ASSOCIATIONS

AUSTRALIA
- AUSTRALIAN YACHTING FEDERATION
- Locked Bag 806, Milsons Point, NSW 2061, Australia
- E-mail: ausyacht@ausport.gov.au
- Website: www.ausailing.org

CANADA
- WINDSURF CANADA
- Canadian Yachting Association, Portsmouth Olympic Harbour, 53 Yonge Street, Kingston, Ontario K7M 6G4, Canada
- Website: www.sailing.ca

CANARY ISLANDS
Auspices of Spanish Sailing Federation
- SPANISH SAILING FEDERATION
- Luis de Salazar 12, 28002 Madrid, Spain
- E-mail: info@rfev.es
- Website: www.rfev.es

FROM THE WAVE-LASHED BEACHES OF ARUBA TO EXOTIC ZANZIBAR, ENTHUSIASTS FOLLOW THE WINDS AND THE WAVES ACROSS THE GLOBE.

CARIBBEAN

- CARIBBEAN SAILING ASSOCIATION
- PO Box 155, Jolly Harbour, Antigua, Caribbean

CHINA

- CHINESE YACHTING ASSOCIATION
- 9 Tiyuguan Road, Beijing 100763
- E-mail: lquanhai@public-3bta.net.cn

CYPRUS

- CYPRUS YACHTING ASSOCIATION
- PO Box 51813, Limmasol, Cyprus
- E-mail: cya@dial.cylink.com.cy

DENMARK

- DANISH SAILING ASSOCIATION
- Idrattens Hus/House of Sports, DK-2605 Brondby, Denmark
- E-mail: mia@sejlsport.dk

EGYPT

- GYBEMASTERS
- Moon Beach, Sinai

FRANCE

- FRENCH SAILING FEDERATION
- 55 Avenue Kleber, 75784 Paris, Cedex 16, France
- E-mail: barbierm@compuserve.com
- Website: www.ffv.fr

GERMANY

- GERMAN WINDSURFING ASSOCIATION
- Grundenstrasse 18, 22309 Hamburg

IRELAND

- IRISH SAILING ASSOCIATION
- 3 Park Road, Dun Laughaire, County Dublin, Ireland
- E-mail: Isa@iol.ie
- Website: www.sailing.org/isa

ITALY

- ITALIAN SAILING FEDERATION
- Corte Lambruschini, Piazza Borgo Pila 40, Torre A – 16 Piano, 16129 Genova, Italy
- E-mail: federvela@federvela.it
- Website: www.federvela.it

MEXICO

- MEXICAN WINDSURFING ASSOCIATION
- E-mail: pedros@sureste.com

NETHERLANDS

- NETHERLANDS WINDSURFING ASSOCIATION
- KNWU, PO Box 87, 3980 CB Bunnik, Netherlands

NEW ZEALAND

- NEW ZEALAND YACHTING
- PO Box 90 900, Auckland Mail Centre, Auckland
- E-mail: mail@yachting.org.nz

SINGAPORE

- SINGAPORE BOARD SAILING ASSOCIATION
- PA East Coast Sea Sports Club, 1390 East Coast Parkway, Singapore
- E-mail: bsasing@mbox2.singnet.com.sg
- Website: www.singnet.com.sg/~bsasing

SOUTH AFRICA

- WINDSURF AFRICA (NATIONAL BODY)
- Private Bag X16 Auckland Park, 2006 Johannesburg

SPAIN

- SPANISH SAILING FEDERATION
- Luis de Salazar 12, 28002 Madrid
- E-mail: info@rfev.es
- Website: www.rfev.es

UNITED KINGDOM

- ROYAL YACHTING ASSOCIATION
- RYA House, Romsey Road, Eastleigh, Hants SO50 9YA, England
- Website: www.rya.org.uk

USA

- US WINDSURFING
- PO Box 978, Hood River, OR 97031
- E-mail: info@uswindsurfing.org
- Website: www.uswindsurfing.org

Glossary

All-round Board or sail that has a wide application for general recreational use.

Batten Fiberglass or carbon rod or tube that is inserted into the 'batten pocket'. The rod or tube tapers towards the mast and helps give the sail its shape and stability.

Beach start A basic method of launching without having to uphaul the sail.

Bearing away Steering the board away from wind.

Belly Depth or 'fullness' of the curve across the sail.

Blasting Sailing in and out on a beam reach. In other words, leave the shore, go out, turn around, and sail back to your departure point.

Broad reach The point of sailing between a beam reach (90° to the wind) and a run (dead downwind). Generally, this is the fastest point of sailing.

Bouyancy aid Any of a number of flotation devices and accessories that help the sailor to keep afloat when in the water.

Carve jibe A high-speed technical turn executed on a short board.

Clew The area of the sail that attaches to the rear end of the boom.

Cringle A metal eyelet in the sail.

Catapult A term used to describe the action when a sailor is suddenly pulled off the board by a strong gust of wind.

Center of effort The balance point of the sail, where the power is most concentrated.

Cross-shore (also known as 'side-shore') The term used to describe the wind when it is blowing either left to right, or right to left across the beach.

Dagger board The dagger board helps the inexperienced beginner to sail closer to the wind, reducing the chances of drifting downwind and away from the starting point.

Dead downwind (also known as 'running') Sailing with the wind blowing down the length of the board, while the sailor holds the sail out in front of them.

Downhaul The line that attaches the bottom of the sail (tack) to the mast base. On most modern boards, the line passes through a pulley-hook to make tensioning the downhaul easier.

Downhauling The action of tensioning the downhaul line that gives the sail its shape and stability.

Eye of the wind The precise direction from which the wind is blowing.

Foot The bottom area and edge of the sail.

Footsteer When the board is turned by pressure through the feet on the edge of the board.

Flat A term commonly used to describe the set of a sail. A sail that is rigged 'flat' has less power than a full sail.

Freestyle The collective term for performing a number of deft maneuvers.

Flare jibe Jibing a board tightly by sinking and pivoting on its tail.

Grunt A tool used to help tension the downhaul. There are custom products (called Easi-Rigg), but using the harness spreader bar or wooden/metal bar is just as functional.

Harness Seat, waist or chest harnesses all have a hook that allows sailors to 'hook in' to the harness lines attached to the boom and use their body weight — rather than the arms — to balance against the sail.

Head The top of the sail.

Hull The basic board — without the rig.

Jibing Turning the board around, with the tail passing through the eye of the wind.

Leech The trailing edge of the sail.

Leeward The side that faces away from the sail.

Luffing (also known as 'heading wind') Turning the board closer towards the wind.

Mast track The point at which the mast base attaches to the board.

Outhaul The line used to attach the clew to the rear end of the boom. If the sail is 'outhauled', the line is tensioned.

Out of the turn The expression used to describe the end part of a 180° turn, such as tacking or jibing. Looking 'out of the turn' helps sailors to see where they are going and establishes greater awareness of the intended course.

Pitch Dip and raise the bow and stern alternately.

Planing The action when the board is travelling at speed and results in much of the hull rising out of the water as the board accelerates.

Powered up Enough power in the sail to support the sailor in the harness. This usualy refers to planing conditions when boards are travelling at high speed.

Rake The term used to describe the position when the sail is inclined back towards the tail. This usually makes the board head upwind.

Reaching Sailing at approximately 90° to the wind. Most windsurfers spend their time on the water 'reaching' in and out.

Rig The collective term that incorporates the sail, boom, mast and mast base.

Sailing pretty tight Sailing quite close to or into the wind. This usually refers to a situation in which the dagger board is down and the windsurfer is trying to move upwind – possibly back to the shore after having drifted downwind.

Sailing quite broad Sailing away from the wind on a broad reach, usually with the dagger board up. This is when the board travels at its fastest.

Set The term used to describe the action of rigging a sail. Sails are 'set' using outhaul and downhaul. The 'set' can range between 'flat' and 'full'.

Sheeting in The action of pulling the clew of the sail closer to the centerline of the board. This generally increases power and speed.

Slalom Common style of high-speed, short-board racing.

Spreader bar The metal and aluminum bar that attaches to the harness, 'spreading' the pull from the harness lines across the sailor's hips for additional comfort.

Tack Turning the board around 180°, with the nose of the board passing through the eye of the wind.

Trim Finely adjusting the sail to the wind direction.

Uphaul The rope used to pull the rig clear of the water. An action known as 'uphauling'.

Water start The maneuver in which the sailor is lifted out of the water and onto the board by the power of the wind in the sail.

Windward The side of the board onto which the wind is blowing.

FOR ARDENT ENTHUSIASTS, FEW OTHER WATERSPORTS CAN COMPARE TO THE THRILL AND ADVENTURE OF WINDSURFING.

Index

Photographic Credits

E. Aeder: pp 40, 73; **Allsport/Touchline (Graham Chadwick):** p 77 (bottom); **Peter Bentley:** pp 77 (top), 91 (bottom); **Bic Sport/Jono Knight:** pp 11, 35; **David Eberlin:** p 26 (top); **Rob Jewell:** p 2; **Simon Miles/SBW:** pp 8 (top), 10 (bottom left), 12, 20, 21, 22, 34 (bottom), 65, 67, 69, 70, 71, 76 (top right), 82, front cover; **Mistral/Ulli Seer:** pp 18 (top), 26 (bottom), 54 (top), 86 (bottom left); **Mistral/Darrell Wong** p 78 (bottom); **Presse Sports/Jutta Mueller:** p 92; **SSM/John Carter:** pp 10 (top), 17 (bottom right), 23 (center right and bottom right), 33, 66 (top), 72 (bottom), 74, 75, 80 (bottom), 85, 86 (top), 88 (bottom), 89 (bottom), 90 (right), 91 (top); **SSM/ Williams:** pp 4/5, 6/7, 72 (top), 76 (top), 88 (top), 90 (left); **Alex Williams:** pp 16, 27 (right). **Images supplied courtesy of the individual manufacturers:** pp 13, 15 (center left), 17 (bottom left, center and top right), 27 (left), 34 (top), 76 (bottom left and right), 79, 87.